Psychology 101½

Psychology 101½

The Unspoken Rules for Success in Academia

Robert J. Sternberg

American Psychological Association

Washington, DC

Published by
American Psychological Association
750 First Street, NE
Washington, DC 20002
www.apa.org

To order
APA Order Department
P.O. Box 92984
Washington, DC 20090-2984
Tel: (800) 374-2721; Direct: (202) 336-5510
Fax: (202) 336-5502; TDD/TTY: (202) 336-6123
On-line: www.apa.org/books/
E-mail: order@apa.org

In the U.K., Europe, Africa, and the Middle East, copies may be ordered from
American Psychological Association
3 Henrietta Street
Covent Garden, London
WC2E 8LU England

Typeset in ITC Garamond and Adobe Birch by
World Composition Services, Inc., Sterling, VA

Printer: Automated Graphic Systems, White Plains, MD
Cover Designer: Anne Masters Design, Washington, DC
Technical/Production Editor: Casey Ann Reever

The opinions and statements published are the responsibility of the authors, and such opinions and statements do not necessarily represent the policies of the American Psychological Association.

Library of Congress Cataloging-in-Publication Data

Sternberg, Robert J.
Psychology 101 1/2 : the unspoken rules for success in academia /
  Robert J. Sternberg.
    p. cm.
Includes bibliographical references and index.
ISBN 1-59147-029-3 (pbk. : alk. paper)
    1. Psychology—Study and teaching (Higher) 2. Psychology—Study and teaching (Graduate) I. Title: Psychology one hundred one and a half.
II. Title: Psychology one hundred and one and a half. III. Title.
BF77.S68 2003
150'.71'1—dc21

2003002006

British Library Cataloguing-in-Publication Data
A CIP record is available from the British Library.

Printed in the United States of America
First Edition

To Endel Tulving, Gordon Bower, Wendell Garner,
and my colleagues at PACE

Contents

CONTENTS

CONTENTS

Preface

TRAINING FOR AN ACADEMIC CAREER involves a great deal of preparation with regard to the subject matter of the discipline and even with the methods used in the discipline, but relatively little preparation regarding the real challenges one faces in an academic career: namely, how to deal with oneself, others, one's work, and the field as a whole. For this reason, careers are made and broken often not on what one learned in graduate school or as a young professional, but on what one should have learned but did not. Worse, those who fail to reach their goals often are puzzled as to what went wrong and receive little or no satisfaction by asking others.

The goal of this book is to provide advice to young (and perhaps some not so young) psychologists in academia—graduate students, postdoctoral fellows, junior faculty, and perhaps some not-so-junior faculty. I attempt to do so by providing some of the "tacit knowledge" that can and often does mean the difference between success and failure in a career. By tacit knowledge, I refer to knowledge that is typically informal (as opposed to the formal knowledge taught in classrooms), procedural (as opposed to the declarative knowledge that constitutes the stuff of lectures and texts), and unverbalized or hidden. Although tacit knowledge can be brought out in the open, it often is not, with the result that people participating in a system that is rich in tacit knowledge usually need to discover the knowledge for themselves—if they can.

I believe there are several reasons why a book such as this one needed to be written. First, the book is relevant to psychologists in any field and, potentially, at any level of advancement. Second, although the kinds of lessons presented in the book are very important to personal and career success, they often are not taught nor even learned informally. Third, this is the kind of book that I hope will have a long shelf life: It should not go out of date as fashions and fads in psychology change.

I believe most of the lessons in this book—perhaps all of them—are relevant in any field of academic inquiry but that because the examples are all from psychology, the primary audience will be psychologists and future psychologists. Other aspiring and young academics may constitute a second audience. A third audience is senior faculty who realize that despite their seniority, they still have a lot to learn (and who doesn't?). They may also want to use the book as a basis for their own mentorship of younger people.

I believe the book may be of use for first-year proseminars and also for courses on professional issues that are taught in some psychology departments. The lessons are presented in no particular order. Originally, I tried to organize them by themes, but the truth is that in academia so many things are interrelated that it is difficult to isolate them from each other arbitrarily. Each lesson is presented in a way so as to make four basic points, although the format is varied to preserve the interest of the text: (a) the lesson, (b) how and where I learned it, (c) why it is important, and (d) one or more concrete examples of it. All of the concrete examples are real and from my career or those of other people I have known personally.

In using this book, keep three things in mind. First, there is no recipe for success that works for everyone. Learning the lessons in this book will help you get where you want to go. But it will not get you there. *You* have to get yourself there. Second, do not let yourself get discouraged by the large number of ways in which you need improvement. I have been in the field 27 years, and I still have innumerable ways in which I can improve. Self-improvement is a lifelong "course," not a quick fix. Finally, look at the 101 ½ lessons in this book not as obstacles, but as opportunities. They provide you with shortcuts to attaining your goals, whatever those goals may be.

I am grateful to the members of the Center for the Psychology of Abilities, Competencies, and Expertise (PACE Center) at Yale and to Gail Illman for their detailed comments and suggestions on the original version of the manuscript.

Preparation of this book was supported by Grant REC-9979843 from the National Science Foundation, by a government grant under the Javits Act Program (Grant No. R206R000001) as administered by the Office of Educational Research and Improvement, U. S. Department of Education, by Contract DASW01-00-K-0014 from the Army Research Institute, and by a grant from the W. T. Grant Foundation. Grantees undertaking such projects are encouraged to express freely their professional judgment. This book, therefore, does not necessarily represent the positions or the policies of the U.S. government or the W. T. Grant Foundation, and no official endorsement should be inferred.

This book is dedicated to my mentors, Endel Tulving (my undergraduate advisor), Gordon Bower (my graduate advisor), and Wendell Garner (a senior colleague who influenced me significantly during my first years as an assistant professor at Yale) and to my colleagues at the PACE Center at Yale, who continually teach me new lessons about myself, others, careers, and life.

Psychology 101½

❧ Lesson 1 ❧

Don't Believe Things Just Because Other People Do

ENDEL TULVING HAS MADE A CAREER of defying people's expectations. When most people believed that merely repeating a word would have to increase recall for that word because increased frequency should result in increased retrieval of the word, Tulving (1966) showed that under certain circumstances, increased repetitions of a word could actually impair recall of a word. When most people believed that recognition memory must be better than recall memory, Tulving performed a series of experiments showing that recall memory could be better than recognition memory (Tulving & Thomson, 1973). Perhaps Tulving's most surprising finding was that under certain circumstances, forced-choice picture recognition can be *higher* when distractors are more similar to targets rather than less similar (Tulving, 1981). In other words, if you have to say which of two pictures you have seen before, you would expect it to be easier to give the correct response if the distractor (incorrect) picture is less similar to the target rather than more similar. In this way, it should be easier to distinguish the picture you saw from the impostor picture. Tulving showed that having a more similar distractor can actually make the task easier!

A major lesson I learned from Tulving was that just because many people believe something does not make it true; on the contrary, Tulving has tended throughout his career to be skeptical of things that a lot of people believe.

When I was young—back in the 1950s—there was a time when every kid had a hula hoop. If you did not have one, you were, well, nobody. A few years later everyone had

3

put away his or her hula hoop. The new fad was yo-yos. Everyone just had to have a yo-yo. If you didn't, horrible things would happen to you, at least in your social circles. Hula hoops never came back—not yet, anyway. Yo-yos did— briefly—but today scooters are the rage, although the fad has already passed its peak, and the chances are that a lot of garages and basements are already storing never-again-to-be-used scooters.

Many of us who entered scientific careers did so because we thought we were putting the fad-purchasing mentality behind us. We may have been nonconformists as children—and perhaps as adults as well—and therefore have found the practice of "keeping up with the Joneses" somewhat repugnant.

Yet, there may be some cancellation principle at work, whereby when one puts a bunch of nonconformists together into a field, their nonconformities somehow cancel each other out. As Thomas Kuhn (1970) argued, science seems to survive, to a large extent, on the kind of conformity many of its practitioners thought they had rejected. Are there risks to just following the crowd?

1. *Ephemeral fashions.* The first risk is that what you do will not look nearly as attractive in the long run as it does in the short run. For example, when I was in graduate school, semantic memory was a very fashionable thing to study. But a few years later, it was history. Just a few years ago, connectionism was very much an "in thing." Today, it maintains a robust army of followers and developers but does not have the zip of a few years back. Work that at one time may appear to be in *the* area may later appear to be in *that* area—an area that no longer is au courant.

2. *Quality of work.* Suppose you have a choice between two candidates for a job opening: one in the 90th percentile of her field and the other in the 60th. All other things being equal, you will probably go for the one in the 90th

percentile. But all other things are never quite equal. Suppose that one is in a current "hot" area (e.g., cognitive neuroscience) and the other in a "cooler" area (e.g., non-biological study of episodic memory). Which one will you pick? Now, think about yourself. If your heart is in one thing but the fad is in another, would you rather do your very best work in the nonfaddish field or do so-so work in the faddish field? What is important is to do your best work.

3. *Encouraging choice on the basis of fashion rather than passion.* Many job-hunters go where the jobs are. If they see that job openings are largely a function of current fashions, then they are likely to want to specialize in these fashions. Areas of research that are important to the field may be neglected, and areas that deserve some but not so much attention may get more work done in them than they merit. Meanwhile, students are studying not what they really want to study, but what they believe they should study to get a job. As a result, they do not optimize on their own creative potential because they are not working in an area that poses the psychological problems that interest them most.

4. *Fueling what may be a foolish fad.* In 2001, the United States experienced a painful dot-com crash. The crash caused a severe dislocation in the U.S. economy and also in many people's future plans. Why did so few people see it coming? Perhaps one could forgive the young "dot-commers," who had not experienced before the ups and downs of the business cycle. But many of the people who were caught short were older, experienced investors who perhaps should have known better. Employers kept hiring people for whom there was a short-term but not a long-term demand and then later laid many of them off. Similarly, in academic psychology, older, more experienced psychologists should recognize that trends are—well—trends. They come and they go. It is embarrassing to the field of psychology—as it was in the technology field—when senior people in the field act as though a fad never will end.

5

5. *Choking off important areas of research.* At the same time that fads may distort the field by overemphasizing some areas or methods of research, it may choke off other areas or methods that do not deserve this fate. There is a pecking order of prestige of fields, whether we acknowledge it or not. It is probably easier, on average, to get a prestigious job if one works in the field of perception rather than in the field of creativity, or in the field of prejudice rather than of love. Studying certain areas that are not in fashion may end up costing one the job one hopes for. It may be, in some cases, that certain fields do have intrinsically more value than others—for example, perception rather than extrasensory perception. But in choosing people in terms of current pecking orders, we may lose the benefit of research in important fields that are understudied for no other reason than they are not trendy.

6. *Methods rather than substance.* I was recently asked by a department chair if I knew of any strong junior people on the job market who used fMRI techniques (functional magnetic resonance imaging) in their research. I was also told by a colleague that a job advertisement specifically sought a candidate who uses fMRI methods. This approach to hiring is, perhaps, bizarre. Rather than looking for someone who studies a certain problem (e.g., memory or prejudice) or even someone who is in a particular field of psychology (e.g., cognitive psychology or social psychology), one is seeking someone who uses a particular technology in his or her research. But any problem is best studied through the use of converging operations—that is, a confluence of methods. What message do we send to students when we hire on the basis of a technology used in research rather than on the basis of what the person actually studies?

7. *Fundamental values.* Are we, as a field, really about fads? For example, can we tell people that really they were hired not so much because of their scholarly strength but because of the faddishness of the kind of research they do? We need to be true to ourselves.

This lesson is not an exercise in playing holier than thou. I had a hula hoop around when I was in first grade. Then I had a yo-yo when I was in sixth grade. I do not have a scooter. I hope I have outgrown my need to follow fads. Shouldn't we all?

❧ Lesson 2 ❧

Reinvent Yourself on a Periodic Basis

WHEN I WAS A TEENAGER, I observed that some vocalists seemed to have careers that went on and on, and others had careers that came and went like a fleeting drumbeat. Diana Ross, Barbra Streisand, and Placido Domingo would be examples of the former, whereas Johnny Mathis, Paul Anka, and Bobbie Vinton would be examples of the latter. What's the difference?

I believe that the difference is in the two groups of artists' skills in reinventing themselves. Some artists keep discovering new acts. In recent years, Madonna has been an example. But Juice Newton, a soft-rock vocalist who experienced a brief fling with stardom, has not had so many new acts. Among visual artists, Pablo Picasso was among the best in rein-venting himself.

Scientists are no different from artists in this regard. Some of the greatest scientists of the past 50 years—Richard Nisbett, Michael Posner, Roger Shepard, Robert Zajonc, for example—have each had what seem to be many careers rather than just a single one. Nisbett, for example, has studied weight control, human inference processes, teaching statistical thinking, honor and violence, and cross-cultural cognition, among many other things. As a result, his career has never gone stale. At the same time, I have seen many scientists who essentially had one idea and were unable to move beyond it. They either tried to reinvent themselves and failed to do so or, more likely, never even tried. They became mired in their own bog. Don't let it happen to you.

❧ Lesson 3 ❧

Go Your Own Way and the Rewards Will Follow

I RECENTLY EDITED A BOOK on *Psychologists Defying the Crowd* (Sternberg, 2002b). The main point of the book is that creative scientists defy the scientific establishment (Sternberg, 1999a; Sternberg & Lubart, 1995). Such scientists may choose to go their own way with respect to theory, research paradigm, philosophical orientation, or subject matter studied. The risks can be great because the cost of such defiance can be rejected articles, unfunded grant proposals, and, in extreme cases, scientific oblivion. Yet, these scientists—individuals such as Wundt, Freud, and Binet—are often and perhaps usually the ones whose work lives on, whereas the work of those scientists who pandered to existing scientific tastes often (although certainly not always) dies with them.

For young scientists in general and for psychologists in particular, the pressure to conform is great. Rejection rates of journals and granting agencies in psychology are among the highest of any field, reviews by referees sometimes the most vicious. Radically nonconforming work is less likely to be accepted. Young scientists typically have only 5 to 7 years before they reach an "up or out" decision for tenure, and even graduate students may find that working within the research paradigms of their mentors is substantially safer than finding their own way when they seek a letter of recommendation.

Scientists who defy the crowd are rare because there is so much pressure to conform. In the short term, the rewards of conformity are great: easier job placement or promotion, better funding, easier acceptance of journal submissions and book proposals, approbation of colleagues, and a sense of affiliation with the crowd. In the long run, however, the rewards of creative nonconformity may be substantially greater.

There are many good examples in my book of psychologists who defied the crowd and won (Sternberg, 2002b; see also Sternberg, Kaufman, & Pretz, 2002; Sternberg & Lubart, 1995; for examples from other fields). Ellen Berscheid was pilloried by a senator, by many in the press, and even by some of her colleagues for having the audacity to study love in a scientific way. She received death threats. Today she has won most of the major awards in psychology, including the American Psychological Association (APA) Distinguished Scientific Contribution Award, for her landmark contributions to the psychology of interpersonal attraction. Indeed, together with Elaine Hatfield, she practically originated the field of the social psychology of love, as we now know it. For quite a while, John Garcia was unable to publish some of his work on conditioning in any major journal. His findings that learning could occur in one trial and that the nature of the reinforcement *does* matter were so controversial that many psychologists refused to accept them. He, too, later became a winner of the APA Distinguished Scientific Contribution Award. The point is that resisting the temptation to follow the crowd can be a winning strategy if one has the right ideas and, perhaps just as important, the guts to stick with them.

The biggest problem, of course, is knowing *when* to defy the crowd and when not to. There is no ironclad set of rules for knowing. However, here are some tips that may be useful. The more questions you answer "yes," the more likely it is you should defy the crowd.

- Is the issue a matter of principle?
- Is the issue one about which you care deeply?
- Is the issue an important one—for you, for others, for science, for society?

- Have you considered all possible issues in coming to your position?
- Do you have credible arguments to support your position?
- Will there be significant adverse consequences if you fail to defy the crowd?
- Are you confident of the rightness of your position?
- Will your conscience bother you if you fail to defy the crowd?
- Is there any reasonable chance of recruiting others to take your position?
- Are you willing to fight for your position, come what may?

❧ Lesson 4 ❧

Decide What Is Important to You, and Then Be True to It

I LEARNED THIS LESSON from Wendell Garner, my mentor when I was a junior faculty member at Yale. It's important to follow this lesson because if you let the important things go— the things you really stand for—soon you may find yourself standing for nothing. The things that are really important to you largely define who you are, and in letting go of them, in an important sense, you give up on yourself.

During my fifth year as an assistant professor, I was being considered for an appointment as a tenured associate professor in the Department of Psychology at Yale. Yale, like many other universities, seeks opinions from external referees to guide it in the rendering of tenure decisions. Thus, it was important to impress not only senior people within the university, but also, senior people outside of it.

I began to hear rumors that some of the external letters that were coming in were skeptical about my defining myself as being in the field of human intelligence. Fields within psychology, as within any science, have different levels of prestige, and intelligence has tended over the years to be toward the bottom of the ladder of prestige. One can see this by the fact that there are few graduate programs in human intelligence and almost no jobs defined as ones in the field of human intelligence.

When I heard about the referees' letters, I felt close to a state of panic. How could I have made such a dumb decision regarding the field in which I worked? I spoke to Wendell Garner, my informal senior-faculty mentor, and told him that

12

I thought I had made a dreadful mistake. I had realized that I could have done exactly the same work I had been doing all along, but called it something else. For example, I might have called my work research on "thinking" or "problem solving" or even "reasoning," all of which were higher in prestige than "human intelligence," and all of which could have provided a sensible and safe label for my work.

Garner heard me out, and then gave me some of the best advice I ever have gotten. He said, in essence, that I had entered psychology and then come to Yale with the mission of wanting to make a difference to the field of intelligence. Now I was afraid that this mission would cost me my job. I was right, he said, in thinking that it might cost me my job. But the right thing for me to do was to continue to define myself as being in the field of intelligence. The reason was that my mission was extremely important to me—it was what I cared about—and so I had to follow it, even if it cost me my job.

I realized he was right and continued to define myself as being in the field of intelligence. And I got tenure. I might not have. But I realized that there was no room for compromise on something so important to me, and that this was the only position I could take.

During the course of a career, there are always temptations to abandon things you deeply believe in. You may deeply believe in teaching but find that most of the rewards are for research, or vice versa. You may deeply believe in a certain approach to a problem that just happens not to be popular in your department. The temptations to sell out are enormous, and the rewards seemingly large. But selling out may or may not get one the rewards one seeks; it always loses one the most important reward of all, a sense of personal identity and integrity.

13

❧ Lesson 5 ❧

Find Your Mission and Define Success in Terms of Realizing It

ALTHOUGH I HAVE STUDIED intelligence for many years, it is only relatively recently that I have come to define intelligence not in terms of some arbitrary societal definition of success, but rather, in terms of personal definitions within a sociocultural context. In particular, I define "successful intelligence" (Sternberg, 1997a, 1999b) as the ability to achieve success, according to one's own definition of success, within one's sociocultural context. The message of this definition is that there is no one definition of success that works for everyone, either across societies or even within these societies. We all need to decide what success means for us. For some people, it might be as a musician, for others, as a plumber, for others, as a househusband, for others, as a mother, and for others, as a psychologist. If you are reading this book, there is a good chance that at least part of your definition of success is in terms of being a psychologist.

But it turns out that there is no one definition of success even for psychologists. Some psychologists succeed by being superb teachers, others by being superb researchers, others by being superb practitioners, and still others in other ways. And within each of these categories, there are many ways to succeed. We all need to find our own path. This need is why it is so important for mentors not to judge their mentees in terms of the extent to which the mentees reach the goals of the mentors, but rather, in terms of the extent to which the mentees reach their own goals.

14

Over the course of a 27-year career, I have supervised many graduate students and postdoctoral students and, of course, undergraduate students as well. Some of my students have become academics; others have become management consultants, publishers' representatives, marketing consultants, statistical consultants, and so on. I view their success in terms of my own theory, which is to say, in terms of the extent to which they have furthered the accomplishment of their own goals. I would rather have a student become a successful management consultant than an unsuccessful academic (however the student may define success in his or her subsequent career).

In the course of your career, there will be many people who will try to set your goals for you. My advice is, well, to listen to their advice. But no one can set your goals for you. That is something you have to do. There will be all kinds of pressure to listen to and follow the advice of others. Resist the temptation to succumb. Do what you believe is right for you: There is no other way in which you can be and continue to become yourself.

❧ Lesson 6 ❧

Be Proactive, Not Reactive

THERE IS A KIND OF PERSON one finds quite often who almost never makes money in the stock market: This is the person who waits to see where others are investing and then follows them. For example, they will eagerly buy the investment newsletter for a particular year, find out who the winners of last year's mutual funds investment "derby" were, and then buy shares in that mutual fund. The next year, of course, the fund will almost never do as well (a data point that could be predicted by statistical regression alone). By following the pack, they somehow almost always manage to come out with the short end of the stick.

Professional lives show the same trends. There is a large group of people who are always waiting to see who jumps in what pool, and then they jump in after several people whom they admire jump in first. By the time they jump in, however, the pool is crowded, not so clear, and perhaps even dirty! The people who are merely reactive rarely come out well ahead.

When students arrive on campus—starting as an undergraduate student, or a graduate student, or a postdoctoral student, or even, sometimes, as a faculty member—one of the biggest mistakes I've seen them make is to wait for things to happen. They arrive and expect that the university will provide some series of stimuli, that they will respond to these stimuli, and that by doing so properly, they will be on the path toward greatness. Nothing could be further from the truth. What a university does, typically, is to provide an environment in which there are resources and opportunities there for the asking. But more often than not, the opportunities do not just come to you. Rather, you must seek them out. And often you must *create* the opportunities. In other words, you need to be proactive rather than reactive.

I ran for president of the American Psychological Association twice. The first time I was reactive. I waited for things to happen. They didn't—other than my losing. The second time I was proactive. I created a campaign, with the help of my friends and colleagues. Everyone worked together with a common goal. I—or really, we as a group—won. The lesson was simple: Good things do not come to those who wait. Good things come to those who go after good things and make them happen. Decide what you want, then go for it. Don't wait for it to come to you.

❧ Lesson 7 ❧

Never Get Stuck on Seeing a Problem in Just One Way

PEOPLE SOMETIMES GET STUCK on seeing a problem in one particular way. They start hitting their head against the wall, trying to figure out a solution to their problem as they define it. Don't get stuck. Always ask whether there is some way to redefine your problem. A good example of redefining a problem is summed up in the story of an executive at one of the biggest automobile companies in the Detroit area. The executive held a high-level position, and he loved his job and liked the money he made on the job. However, he despised the person he worked for, and because of this, he decided to find a new job. He went to a headhunter, who assured him that a new job could be easily arranged. After this meeting the executive went home and talked to his wife, who was teaching a unit on redefining problems as part of a course she was teaching on Intelligence Applied (Sternberg, 1986; Sternberg & Grigorenko, in press). The executive realized that he could apply what his wife was teaching to his own problem. He returned to the headhunter and gave the headhunter his boss's name. The headhunter found a new job for the executive's boss, which the boss—having no idea of what was going on—accepted. The executive then got his boss's job. The executive solved his problem by creatively redefining it.

In my own career, I once was stuck in a particularly irksome situation. I was very concerned about the fact that a certain colleague had what seemed to be a negative perception of my work. I started devoting more and more time to trying to make the colleague see the value of what I was doing. No change. Then I redefined the problem. I realized that it really did not matter a whole lot what this particular colleague thought. I would have liked to change his mind, but I could not. So I went on with my life. Once I redefined the problem, I was fine. The problem was not how to please the person; it was to put the person and his or her opinion of me aside and move on.

❧ Lesson 8 ❧

Realize That You Will Not Succeed in Your Relations With Everyone

DURING MY CAREER, I have advised several dozen undergraduate students, graduate students, and postdoctoral students. Most of the relationships have gone smoothly. Some have not. For one reason or another, I just did not hit it off with the student, or vice versa. On such occasions, either the student has found another mentor on his or her own initiative, or I have suggested that the student might want to look for another advisor.

When relationships with mentees have failed, I have typically felt some degree of distress. Although I know that not all such relationships can work, I have felt partially responsible! But we all need to recognize that we cannot expect to relate effectively to everyone we encounter. Some relationships we have to "write off," although sometimes with regret. I usually try hard to get relationships to work, but I also recognize that there comes a point when one just has to give up.

I once had a graduate-student advisee whom I felt to be quite brilliant. I tried to serve as a mentor to him, but he never seemed to listen to me. I felt as though I was a figurehead mentor, in that he always seemed to feel he knew better than I did. Eventually, I suggested he find another mentor. He needed to be advised by someone whose advice he respected, and I needed to have a student who at least listened to me, even if he disagreed.

In his case, as in others, I have had to admit that the chemistry between a student and myself just was not there.

20

It is to the student's advantage to find someone with whom he or she is comfortable, and to my advantage not to mentor a student whom I cannot really benefit very much. So first we try to work things out, but if we just cannot do so, we both have other options.

❧ Lesson 9 ❧

Realize the Importance of Delaying Gratification

PART OF BEING SUCCESSFUL means being able to work on a project or task for a long time without immediate or interim rewards. Rewards are not always immediate; however, there usually are benefits to delaying gratification. The fact of the matter is that, in the short term, people are often ignored when they do creative work or even punished for doing it.

Many people believe that they should be rewarded immediately for good performance, and that it is always reasonable to expect quick rewards. Not so.

In psychology, you often have to wait for rewards. The greatest rewards are often those that are delayed. I can relate to the concept of delayed gratification, as one of the greatest rewards of my own life has yet to come. Some years ago I contracted with a publisher to develop a test of intelligence based on my theory of intelligence (Sternberg, 1985). Things were going well until the president of the company left and a new president took over. Shortly after that, my project was canceled. The company's perception was that there was not enough of a potential market for a test of intelligence founded on my theory of analytical, creative, and practical abilities. My perception was that the company and some of its market was stuck in the past, endlessly replicating the construction and use of the kinds of tests that had been constructed and used since the turn of the twentieth century. From my point of view, it is hard to find an industry less creative than the testing industry, at least given the rate of innovation they have shown to date.

Some years later, we are still working to find a way that others can use the test. It is a difficult exercise in delay of gratification. But I try to practice what I preach, and so I wait for the day when the test will see the light of day and make a difference to children's lives.

❧ Lesson 10 ❧

Surmount Obstacles Flexibly

WHEN I WAS VERY YOUNG, I became interested in intelligence and intelligence testing as a result of my own poor scores on intelligence tests. As a seventh grader at the age of 13, I decided it would be interesting to do a science project on intelligence testing. I found the Stanford-Binet Intelligence Scales in the adult section of the local library and started giving the test to friends.

This decision proved not to be among the better decisions I have made in my life. The first person to whom I decided to give the test was a girl in whom I was romantically interested. At the time, I was somewhat shy, and thought— as a result of high social intelligence, no doubt—that giving the girl an intelligence test would help break the ice. I was wrong. A practical piece of advice, therefore, is that if you are ever romantically interested in someone, giving the person an IQ test is not a good way to begin a relationship with that person.

The next person to whom I decided to give the test was a fellow I had known from Cub Scouts. Unfortunately, that was not such a hot choice either. Unbeknownst to me, my friend suffered from a severe mental illness. Well, maybe it wasn't really a mental illness. He was a tattletale. My friend tattled to his mother, who reported me to the junior high school guidance counselor. Unfortunately, being a tattletale appeared to be contagious. The guidance counselor reported me to the head school psychologist. The head school psychologist spoke to me and threatened to burn the book that contained the test if I ever brought it into school again. He suggested I find another interest. Had I done so, I never would have done all the work I have done on intelligence, which has meant a great deal to my life, and, I hope, something to the world. His opinion presented a major obstacle to me, especially as an early adolescent. However, because I surmounted that obstacle, I have been able to do research on intelligence, which has been very fulfilling for me.

Obstacles do not go away when one grows older. Indeed, to the extent one is creative and defies the crowd, obstacles are likely to increase. They can be of different kinds at different points in a career. For example, I have had periods when one article after another has gotten rejected: It has seemed as though my name on an article doomed the article to failure before I even wrote it. At other times, I have had strings of grant proposals rejected. I have wondered why I even bothered to write them when they all got turned down. Eventually, things balance out, and some articles start getting accepted and some grants start getting funded.

Some obstacles are immediate ones. One of the things I have discovered is that when one gives a talk, including an important one such as a job talk, anything can go wrong. I have confronted overhead projectors with burned-out bulbs and no replacements available, PowerPoint setups that I was assured would work but that nevertheless did not work, microphones that were underpowered, rooms with layouts and furnishings that seemed to have been stolen from horror movies, and worse. Sometimes I have been told that the audience will be knowledgeable, and found out quickly that they are not; other times I have been told that the audience will know little, and they have been experts.

Probably the worst was when I went to a university in the Boston area with my intelligence slides, arrived 20 minutes before the talk, and saw a poster advertising my talk on "The Nature of Love." My host asked me whether I would like to use the 20 minutes to prepare, and I assured him I did. Basically, I had 20 minutes to generate a talk, and obviously audiovisual aids were out of the question.

The point is that, in the face of obstacles, the key is to be *flexible*. When I go to a talk, I try to have two methods of presentation ready. If PowerPoint fails, I have overheads as backups. Or if all projection fails, I can give my talk without any audiovisuals at all. I have a rough outline of the talks I give in my head, so that, in an emergency, I can give an approximation to that talk if I have to, even if I don't have the slides for it. It will not be a great approximation, but it will get me through.

Two interviews of job candidates stick out in my mind. In one, the interviewee dropped her slides right before the talk. They became hopelessly out of order. She gave a great talk anyway, and got the job. In the other case, a PowerPoint setup failed. The woman simply would not start her talk until the PowerPoint setup was fixed. The result was that she lost 20 minutes of her hour waiting for the setup to work. The first candidate got the job; the second did not. I ended up thinking, only half in jest, that we ought to arrange some kind of catastrophe for each speaker, and see how the speaker handles it. If the speaker successfully negotiates the disaster, we hire the person; if not, we don't. After all, a career requires great flexibility; why not find out right from the start if the candidate has it?

I used to wonder, when I was younger, what it is that distinguishes people who succeed in their careers from people who did not. Is it some kind of ability? Some kind of luck? Or what? No doubt, ability and luck both matter. But I am convinced that sheer persistence in the face of obstacles is an awfully large factor in the equation. Over the years, I have seen many people who started off their careers successfully, and then would encounter some kind of problem or other. Those who allowed themselves to be defeated would end up with their careers on hold, or worse, in tatters. They could not take the heat, so they got out of the kitchen. A career in psychology typically is fraught with difficult situations. It is easy to give up at any time. Many people believe that they are the only ones encountering problems—experiencing the loss of a parent, a divorce, a health problem, a string of rejections, or whatever. But the truth is that, at some time or other, many people experience such losses. The question is not whether one will encounter obstacles. One will. The question is what one will do in the face of obstacles. Few attributes are more important than the willingness flexibly to surmount these obstacles, no matter how insurmountable they may seem at the time.

If there is one point this lesson should make clear, it is that, as often as not, the main obstacles to your success are within you. There are any number of ways you can become the greatest obstacle to your own success. You can engage in self-defeating ruminations. You can sabotage yourself by doing work you know is not the best of which you are capable. You can decide that things will not go well, and thereby set them up not to go well.

Seligman (1998) has argued that one of the best predictors of success in life is an optimistic stance. People who are optimistic often create the circumstances whereby their optimism ultimately will be justified; people who are pessimistic often create circumstances that result in defeat. So if you want to reach your goals and defy the obstacles to achieving them, maintain an optimistic stance. It will not guarantee you success. But it will go a long way.

At the same time, there will sometimes be obstacles that you make every effort to surmount, and you just cannot do so. Sometimes there are things we really want in life, and for whatever reason, they are just not attainable, no matter how hard we strive. It is for this reason that, in life, it is important always to have a "Plan B," just in case your "Plan A" fails.

✤ Lesson 11 ✤

Nip Problems in the Bud

INEVITABLY, THERE WILL BE TIMES in your career when a problem is looming and you will be tempted to do nothing about it—to let it go. A lesson I have learned during my career is that often, if you do nothing early on, what starts off as a small problem becomes a big problem later on. It is better to deal with the problem, if at all you can, before it becomes a large one.

I have seen the problem in many different forms. One is personnel. I direct a center where teamwork and positive mutual support are our watchwords. We try very hard to hire people who will be positive and mutually supportive toward each other. But inevitably, it seems, we make mistakes. Someone joins the center who is not a team player and, often, is not a constructive influence either. What's to be done? It is painful to me as a center director, to the administrative staff of the center, and to the person who is not working out. So the administrative staff tries to start quickly pointing out to the individual, in a constructive way, what is not going well. If repeated attempts to encourage the individual to change his or her behavior fail, we counsel the individual into taking another job elsewhere. Or the individual may decide to seek a job elsewhere without such counsel. After all, our center is not the perfect environment for everyone, and there is no shame in finding that the fit just is not there. Whoever makes the decision, I have found that such rapid attention to and remediation of problems is the way to go because the problems only very rarely solve themselves. More often, they get worse over time if nothing is done.

28

One can see the same thing happen to graduate students in our graduate program and assistant professors who are just starting out as junior faculty. You do them no favor by overlooking things and hoping they will learn if you say nothing. In fact, I have found that most people welcome counseling, but may be too shy to request it. Most people want to succeed and are grateful when you help them achieve success.

The same thing that applies to others applies to oneself as well. Sometimes I have seen signs that my relations with a particular individual are going "south." For whatever reason, one interaction does not go so well, then another doesn't, and then another. Soon there is a noticeable chill in our interpersonal relationship. Wherever possible, I have tried to speak with the person as soon as I see things going on the wrong track. Although an attempt to clear the air does not always work, it is surprising, in my experience, how often it does.

✤ Lesson 12 ✤

Don't Take Things Personally

OVER THE COURSE of a career, I have published a large number of articles and books, almost all of which have been peer-reviewed. Sometimes, the peer reviews are not very positive, and may even be rather negative. And sometimes, they are very negative indeed. Editors and grant-panel monitors should never send out these negative, personal attacks, but sometimes they do.

People have a tendency, especially early in a career, to take things personally. I know I did, and at times, I still do. Sometimes it is hard not to. A critique may seem to be directed at you personally, and may even make ad hominem comments. But it is the rare critique that offers nothing of value to you— nothing that you can use to improve your work. I have learned that the best thing to do is absolutely to ignore the personal comments and hostile tone one sometimes encounters, and simply to use the comments as a basis for improving one's work. I think reviewers have, at one time or another, called me every name under the sun. As we used to say when we were kids, "Sticks and stones can break my bones, but words will never hurt me." Well, they only will if we allow them to. In essence, I try to get something that will be useful to me out of a not so pleasant experience. And I usually can. You can, too. Concentrate on the substance and ignore the personal attacks. If the individual writing a personal attack needs psychotherapy to cope with latent hostility, that is not your problem.

There are other contexts in which it is important not to take things personally. Another important one is in dealing with people who come from cultures or subcultures different from your own. Things that you may interpret as somehow directed against you may merely reflect differences in culture.

The cultural difference may be one of international import. For example, I was once in Japan to give lectures, and had a very friendly graduate-student host who seemed to be going out of her way to be accommodating. At some point in the conversation, she started talking about people who were "Aryans." I found myself taken aback. I had, from time to time, felt that some Japanese had not quite taken full responsibility for siding with the Axis powers during World War II, but I was shocked to hear that some people still believed in such racist and scientifically worthless theories as that of an "Aryan" race. I was ready to give her a piece of my mind when I decided that a more tactful approach was called for. I gently told her that there actually was no scientific basis for the belief in an "Aryan" race. Further discussion revealed that the word she had been trying to say was "alien," and that she was using it to refer to people who lived in a foreign country but who were not naturalized citizens. I realized that an expression I had almost taken as a personal affront was simply a mispronunciation caused by the fact that, in the Japanese language, there is no distinction between the "l" and "r" phonemes.

On another occasion, shortly after I arrived in Venezuela for the first time, I was speaking with a young male assistant professor. We were having a very pleasant conversation, but every so often, he would start moving closer to me. I would then discreetly back up, after which he would start moving closer again. I had a moment of panic thinking that he was coming on to me. This was the furthest thing from my mind when I had started what I had hoped would be just a pleasant professional conversation. I eventually hurriedly left. But after spending some time in Venezuela, I realized that I had misinterpreted his actions. In Venezuela as well as some other Latin American countries, the natural distance between speakers is somewhat less than it is in the United States. We each were trying to establish what for us was the normal distance between two conversationalists. I had simply misconstrued his intentions, and lost the opportunity to continue a pleasant conversation.

Cultural differences can apply not only across countries, but also, across parts of a single country, or even psychology departments within a country. During my early years, I gave a colloquium on my intelligence research at a well-regarded psychology department. The audience seemed to take delight in tearing me to shreds. By the time I was done with that talk, I felt like I had been through the shredder, and felt awfully that my talk had gone so horribly wrong. I later learned that it was the custom of this department to treat all their speakers in this way. They viewed their behavior as showing not that they were dismissive, but rather, that they were engaged. By not understanding the cultural context of the department, I misinterpreted their behavior.

The bottom line is that you are almost always better off not taking things personally. Life is too short! Take the substance of what people say, profit from it, and move on.

❧ Lesson 13 ❧

Turn Defeats Into Opportunities

THERE INEVITABLY come times in careers when one experiences what seem like major defeats. As I mentioned above, it is important not to give up. But it is surprising how many times a defeat can be turned into an opportunity if one is willing to use the defeat as a lesson for the future.

The first major defeat I had was pretty early—when I took the introductory psychology course. I was eager to major in psychology because I had done poorly on intelligence tests as a child and I wanted to understand what intelligence was and, hence, why I had done so poorly. So I figured that a psychology major would answer the question for me, and then maybe I could spend my life researching intelligence.

The course did not go well, to say the least. I got a grade of "C" in the course. I was always awful in courses that emphasized straight rote recall, and this course came pretty close to that. Indeed, things went poorly from the start. The professor gave us our first test—actually, it was the first test I took as an undergraduate at Yale—and then, a few days later, handed back the tests with the understanding that we could leave for the Thanksgiving holiday as soon as we got our test paper back. To make matters worse, he handed back the tests in descending order. The test was on a 10-point scale, so he first handed back the 10s, then the 9s, then the 8s, and so on. The scores went down and I eventually came to the conclusion that my paper must have gotten out of order. I might not have gotten a 10, but when he was down past the 7s, it was clear that something was very wrong.

Eventually, the only people left in the room were people who I assumed were not in the psychology course to become

33

great psychologists—and me. Finally, the professor handed me back my test paper, with a "3" written at the top. The professor commented that "there is a famous Sternberg in psychology and it is obvious from your test score that there won't be another one." What a bummer!

My Thanksgiving vacation left me feeling that I did not have much to give thanks for. It was clear that I was not making it in psychology and would have to find another field. After completing the course with the "C," I decided to switch my major to mathematics, another interest of mine. In the second semester, I took an introductory course for mathematics majors, and failed the midterm. The mathematics professor suggested that those who had scored below 40 on the midterm drop the course. As I had scored in the mid-30s, I dropped. I decided to switch back to psychology, as a "C" seemed better than an "F."

I decided to turn my defeat into an opportunity: I was going to show the professor—and myself—that I could succeed in psychology. My subsequent grades in psychology were mostly "A's," except for the physiological-psychology course, which also required a great deal of memorization. Moreover, I realized that many people do not learn well from courses that emphasize rote memory, and this defeat became a basis for much of my later work on the psychology of instruction. Thus, my experience motivated me not only to improve my own work in psychology, but also to research and develop ways that would help other people to learn better.

The humiliations do not end as one grows older. Later in my career, after I had received an endowed chair, I was invited by the undergraduate psychology organization at Yale to give a talk to a group of undergraduate psychology majors. Of course I was happy to accept their invitation. I went on the assigned day at the assigned time, and was greeted by the two women who had organized the talk, plus one other individual—someone who was visiting my research group at

Yale. Thus I had a total of one person who was to be in the audience. The undergraduates were very apologetic and said that perhaps their publicity efforts had not been all they could have been. I told them not to worry—that in fact, it was perfectly fine.

What I said was that this experience would be invaluable to me in the future. In the future, if I went to give a talk, and as few as two people showed up, then I would at least have done twice as well as I had done that day. In other words, I doubted I would ever again feel that I had an insufficiently large audience. From time to time, I give a talk, and not so many people show up. I remember back to that day and think that as long as I have more than one person, I'm doing better than I did that day.

In short, the question is not whether you will have defeats; you will. The question is whether you can learn from them and turn them into victories. In many cases, you can. It is up to you to figure out how.

❧ Lesson 14 ❧

Get It in Writing

IWAS IN MY THIRD YEAR as a faculty member at Yale. I knew that the chances of tenure at Yale were remote, so I, like other junior faculty, was on the lookout for other job possibilities. One day, I received a call from a colleague at another institution. As I understood it, he called to offer me a job, and better, it was a job as associate professor with tenure. All I would have to do is visit the institution where he was a faculty member, give a talk (which would be essentially pro forma), and the deal would be done.

I was ecstatic. I had my exit strategy! I told the chair of my department what had happened and Yale began to explore the possibility of giving me very early tenure. A committee was formed to consider this possibility. But for whatever reason, something went wrong. I visited the institution, and no one seemed to take me seriously. My talk was not well attended, and I did not even have a formal talk with the chair. An appointment was set up with a real-estate agent, but the whole thing smelled like a farce. I returned from the trip, depressed and anxious.

I then received a call from another faculty member telling me that I was mistaken: I did not have a tenure offer after all. At that point, I decided to call a faculty member I knew in the department (other than the one who initially called me) and he told me I had a "90% offer." It was all but certain. Time passed; I heard nothing. I decided to call the chair of the department, and he told me that I did not have an offer at that time but that he would get back to me. Eventually he did—to tell me that no offer would be forthcoming.

At that moment, I experienced one of the most severe humiliations I've experienced in my life. I had been "dissed" by the other institution, and Yale was considering me for tenure early based on a competitive offer I did not really have! Of course I had to tell the chair of the department, which was pretty bad. Then things went from bad to worse. He asked me to write a letter requesting that the committee considering me for tenure be disbanded. From his point of view, he was doing the sensible thing: The committee had been formed on the basis of certain information, and that information now had proved to be erroneous. To me, however, his request seemed to be adding insult to injury, and I was reluctant to write such a letter.

I considered leaving Yale to go to a third institution, which seemed interested in me for a tenured position. But when I visited this third institution, I realized that all I was doing was running away from the problem. I went back to Yale, wrote the letter, and to my surprise, found that my colleagues were treating me better, rather than worse, than they had before the ugly incident. They respected the way I had handled the situation, and I established some friendships after the fiasco that might never otherwise have developed.

The upshot of this experience was that I learned an important lesson: Get it in writing. I had thought that the phone call constituted an oral offer. There is no such thing. What you do not have in writing, you simply do not have.

The mistake of believing that what one is told orally counts is not limited to young faculty. I have seen senior faculty think they have job offers they do not have, or think that things promised to them orally once they accept an offer will be delivered. Sometimes the delivery fails because the chair of the department or the higher administration changes. But the bottom line is that one must have things in writing in order to have them at all.

❧ Lesson 15 ❧

Don't Cover Up

I N 2002, A MAJOR SCANDAL evolved among the Catholic clergy involving sexual abuse of minors and—the point to be made here—cover-ups of the abuse. What was amazing to many people about the scandal was that those involved were supposed to be moral authorities and role models. But perhaps there was some reason to expect them to act in ways that were no different from the ways in which others might react. Latané and Darley (1970) found that divinity students were no more likely to help people in distress than were other bystanders.

Cover-ups, of course, are nothing new. Some years ago, Gary Hart, a presidential candidate, was apparently having an extramarital affair with a woman named Donna Rice. Hart not only denied the affair, but also invited reporters to follow him so that they would see there was nothing to their allegations. They did follow him, and photographed him with Donna Rice on the deck of a ship.

There is no room in your career for cover-ups. As a lawyer who defended clients accused of various misappropriations once said, it is usually not the original offense but the cover-up that does people in. No one will live a life free of mistakes. You are far better off facing up to these mistakes than trying to cover for them. At times, you may need to issue an erratum to an article you publish, or admit to a serious mistake in your handling of other people, or worse. Covering up is, in my experience, always a mistake. For this reason, I tell people at the center I direct that, if an error is discovered, it is important to admit to it and face whatever consequences there are immediately, rather than to hope that it will just go away. It may go away, but the chances are greater that it will come back in a much uglier form than if you had admitted the mistake as soon as you made it. I emphasize to people at the Center for the Psychology of Abilities, Competencies, and Expertise (PACE Center) that everything we do in terms of research, finance, or practice must be completely open for inspection.

I have made my own share of mistakes, maybe more than my share. For example, a colleague and I once used a global search and replace on an article to replace one word with another, but failed to realize that we were changing the titles of articles in the references. A colleague pointed out to us that, for some reason, one word had been replaced with the other word in the titles of these articles. If it were one article, perhaps it would not have been so bad. But it was many articles, and so the reference list was seriously flawed. We immediately sent an erratum notice to the journal. We also sent a corrected version of the article to those whom we cited in the article (and who still were living!). It was embarrassing, but better than hoping no one else would notice. If you make a mistake, better to admit it than to cover it up.

❧ Lesson 16 ❧

Actively Seek Out
Guidance and Feedback

MANY GRADUATE STUDENTS go to graduate school expecting to get extensive guidance and feedback, and are surprised when they do not receive it. In my experience, active guidance and feedback are often more the exception than the rule. Similarly, many junior faculty members wait a long time for the guidance that never comes. I learned fairly early in my career not to wait for others to come to me. If you want others' feedback, go to them and actively seek it. You may or may not get it, but at least you will have tried—and you will have been proactive, as you should always try to be.

Although I am now a senior faculty member, I still actively seek out guidance and feedback. Moreover, I seek such information not just from senior colleagues, but from junior colleagues as well. Sometimes, people who are less experienced than oneself see things that more experienced people do not see. Our center at Yale has an electronic mailing list, and sometimes when I have an idea, I will circulate it on the list and ask for guidance. Indeed, this book went on the list for comments! Other times, I will raise the point at a group meeting. I rarely am disappointed. Other people always see things one does not see oneself, if only one lets others comment.

Many of the mistakes that I have made that I have recounted in this book could have been avoided if I had sought feedback from colleagues and mentors. Often, we think we know best, or we do not want to disturb others with our requests for help, or we are in a hurry to get something out.

But it is the rare thing we do that we would not do better were we to receive constructive feedback. Hence, it behooves us to ask others for suggestions and to promise to give suggestions to them when they want them.

❧ Lesson 17 ❧

Avoid Defensiveness

ON ARRIVING AT STANFORD for graduate school, I decided to seek my new graduate advisor's feedback on a paper I had written as an undergraduate. I was quite proud of the paper, and even had presented it at a professional convention in Chicago. A few days later my advisor, Gordon Bower, returned the paper. He told me he had crossed out the areas he thought were weak. I looked at the paper and was horrified to see that he had crossed out almost the entire paper, with comments to match. There was very little left of my original product.

My first reaction was to make an appointment to talk to him to tell him what a terrible mistake he had made. But I decided to think things through a bit more, and as I reflected on his comments, I began to realize that I essentially agreed with the points he had made. By dropping my defensiveness, I had given myself a learning opportunity that I otherwise would not have had.

Sometimes it is hard not to be defensive. I recently received in the mail a critique of my work that ran to almost 100 pages in length. The critique was angry, sarcastic, often ad hominem, and full of attempts at one-upmanship—or at least I saw it that way. I was surprised that it had been accepted for publication, but it had been. So I wrote a reply, and I guess I "lost it." I wrote a very detailed, point-by-point refutation of the critique, defending myself against the numerous charges made in the article criticizing my work.

The reply I wrote was reviewed, and the reviewers were less than enthusiastic about my response. They believed that it came across as defensive and as boring, and that no one would be interested in reading a point-by-point rebuttal to the points that had been made. I realized that the reviewers were right—that no purpose was being served by my replying in such a fashion. I therefore threw out most of my lengthy reply, figuring it had served a purpose of psychological catharsis for me—but little else—and wrote a reply that was more positive and more global.

Over the course of my career, I have observed that students profit in very different degrees from the environment we provide in our department, in our university, and in our center. Some seem to learn a great deal and seriously to improve themselves; others improve relatively little. I think a key difference between the two groups is with regard to their relative levels of defensiveness. Some students use feedback as an opportunity to learn; others seem to learn little from the feedback they receive. I've had students start out fairly far behind who eventually advance in front of others, not necessarily because they are "smarter," at least in a traditional way, but rather because they are willing to take guidance and learn in a nondefensive way. Defensiveness closes you off to growth and, really, to fulfillment of your potential. Thus, you may feel like you are helping yourself in blocking out criticisms or feelings of rejection, but the truth is that you are doing anything but helping yourself.

The need to be nondefensive does not end when one becomes a professional. Learning is a lifelong experience. People who allow themselves to profit from feedback—and even painful criticism—will continue to grow and improve throughout their entire careers.

❧ Lesson 18 ❧

Do What You Believe Is Right

NOT SO LONG AGO, as I mentioned earlier, I decided to run for president of the American Psychological Association and try to win. I had been president of four APA divisions, and thought that I was up to the challenge. Because there are five candidates running in the election, and because all are typically very prominent psychologists, it is difficult to win this election. If one wishes to win, then one has to set one's mind to it and make a serious effort.

Fairly early during the campaign period, a very difficult situation arose in the APA (see Sternberg, 2002a). A well-known psychologist wrote an article that was somewhat critical of the APA. The author of the article received from the action editor what he reasonably believed to be an acceptance of his article, and even a letter congratulating him on the article's acceptance. Then the apparent acceptance was rendered conditional by a higher-level editor who asked the author to make substantial revisions to the article. The author was outraged and sent an e-mail to several individuals expressing his view of events and his outrage.

The e-mail was widely circulated and soon a storm was brewing. Prominent scientists came to the defense of the author and expressed their dissatisfaction with the way the APA had handled the situation. Some of the postings were downright hostile toward the APA and the various officials of the APA involved. The volume and intensity of the e-mail correspondence increased, and members of one prominent psychology department—Harvard—even signed a joint protest letter.

At that point, I found myself in a dilemma. I sympathized with the author: Clearly the handling of his manuscript left much to be desired. Something had gone wrong. But, at the same time, the author had instituted an appeal process, and it seemed to me that he might have waited until the result of the appeal was determined. Moreover, it seemed that even if his point of view was totally justified, psychologists owed it to themselves to hear the point of view of the editor who qualified the original editorial decision. He had not yet been heard from, in part because of the confidentiality that needs to be honored both toward authors and reviewers.

The question was whether I should get myself involved in what had become a very hot argument. Pretty much everyone I spoke to said that I should stay out of it. After all, it was a no-win situation. No matter what I said, I would antagonize a large group of people, and worse, they were people who, under other circumstances, might vote for me. The best thing, it seemed, was just to stay out of it (as the other candidates appeared to be doing).

I gave it a great deal of thought and finally decided I had to speak up, even if it cost me the election. If I did not speak up when I had something to say, then I would feel that, even if I won the election, it would be a hollow victory: I would have won by selling myself out. I decided I would rather say what I believed and lose the election than stay silent at a time of crisis. So I made a series of postings on a widely read listserv.

The results were mixed. Several individuals wrote back to express their agreement with what I had said and their thanks for my having said it. Other individuals wrote back to disagree, in some cases, vociferously. And a few people wrote back to say, in essence, that they would rather vote for the devil than for me. I believe I made more friends than enemies, but who knows? Ultimately, I won the APA election, and was glad I spoke out, because I did what I believed one must do for important issues—do what one believes is right, and let the chips fall where they may.

Sometimes the chips do not fall exactly as one might wish. I once had an employee who was, in my opinion, ineffective in his work and destructive for the morale of the group. When the grant on which he was working came to an end, I terminated his employment, because I had no work I believed he would perform satisfactorily. I knew that the termination would not make him happy. Indeed, the less competent employees are sometimes those who cling most steadfastly to their jobs, because it often is not so easy for them to be hired elsewhere. When I let him go, he decided to file a grievance with the union. At that point, I had to decide whether to subject myself to a grievance hearing—which I definitely did not relish—or somehow try to find work for the employee. I decided to go ahead with the hearing. I simply had nothing that I thought he could do satisfactorily, and so I believed it appropriate that when the grant on which he was working came to an end, so did his employment. I went to the grievance hearing, and won my case. Had I chickened out, I would have been left with an employee whose work was not satisfactory and whose effect on morale was, in my view, deleterious.

❧ Lesson 19 ❧

Make Friends in the Field

I'VE HAD SOME great strokes of luck in my career. I've won a number of awards, I've become a fellow of a number of professional associations, I've been awarded four honorary degrees, and I have been asked to speak in countless places. On the one hand, I've probably earned at least some of these honors! On the other hand . . . .

Behind every award, every fellow nomination, every honorary degree, every speaking engagement, is someone who nominated me. I may have been a good choice, but the truth of the matter is that there are many other people who would have been good choices as well. In each case, someone chose to nominate me, when he or she could have nominated countless other deserving people. It helps to have friends who care about you, because they are the ones most likely to nominate you for things.

At the same time, it is important to remember that friendship is reciprocal. I have nominated many people for various awards. In every case, they were people I felt were eminently qualified for the awards. But the truth is, many people are potentially qualified. Just as friends are more likely to nominate you than to nominate people they do not know, so you are more likely to nominate friends than people you do not know.

Friendship is not just instrumental. Academic psychology is a tough business. You need all the friends you can get, just to stay sane—people with whom to share problems, with whom to speak about things you need to get off your chest, people who mean something to you. I have often felt I would be lost without having some good friends in the field.

47

I think one of the most important aspects of friendships with people in the field is trust. If you cannot trust someone and that person cannot trust you, that person is not your friend, no matter what other things the relationship may have going for it.

Another really important aspect is commitment. A friend is someone who will stick with you when the chips are down. I have seen academia take a brutal toll on some people. But the most brutal toll of all is when their lives start falling apart, and people they thought were their friends all of a sudden find it convenient to make themselves scarce. One person I know was accused—falsely, from what I can tell—of a professional misdeed. What was worse than the false accusation was the speed with which supposed friends and colleagues deserted what they thought was a sinking ship. If you want to be a true friend to a colleague, then you need to commit yourself to that colleague (see Sternberg, 1998b).

✧ Lesson 20 ✧

Be True to Yourself and Let Others Be True to Themselves

WHEN I WAS DECIDING on what to do for a career, I was pretty sure I wanted to be a psychologist. Not entirely sure, in my junior year of college I took a pre-law course on constitutional law and decided that, although it was interesting, it aroused no passion in me. And constitutional law was what I figured would be the most interesting aspect of the law.

Meanwhile, my mother was very interested in my attending law school. She believed, for whatever reason, that I had the right combination of attributes to be a lawyer. My older brother was studying law, and why not have two lawyers in the family? It was hard to tell my mother that I just was not interested in going to law school, but I finally did talk to her.

Three years later I was about to receive my PhD when I had a conversation with my mother. She pointed out that the president of Rutgers University at the time had both a psychology degree and a law degree, and that I could do the same. I told my mother once again that I was not interested in a law degree.

Five years past the PhD, when I was tenured, my mother and I had another conversation. She pointed out that I had now proved to myself that I could be a successful academic psychologist and that it still was not too late to go to law school—that people went even when they were early in other kinds of careers. For the last time, I told her that I would not be going to law school. She never brought up the issue again.

Many of the students in my college graduating class did, in fact, go to law school. I have seen them from time to time at college reunions. My experience with them has been that those who went to law school because they were enthusiastic about it generally are reasonably happy with what they are doing, but those who went because it was the "right thing to do" or because they succumbed to parental or other pressures are, for the most part, quite unhappy and eagerly awaiting retirement. I have had no doubt that I did the right thing not going to law school. And I have made no effort to insist or even encourage my own children to go to law school. But life works in mysterious ways: My daughter started her studies at Yale Law School in the fall!

In working with my children and my students, I try to help them find what interests *them*, whether or not it particularly interests me. Often, their enthusiasm is infectious, and I find myself drawn into new areas of pursuit simply because I allow myself to follow my children rather than always expecting them to follow me.

I often meet students who are pursuing a certain career interest not because it is what they want to do, but because it is what their parents or other authority figures expect them to do. I always feel sorry for such students, because I know that although they may do good work in that field, they almost certainly will not do great work. It is hard for people to do great work in a field that simply does not ignite some kind of passion in them.

Of course, taking this attitude is easier said than done. When my son was young, I was heartened that he wanted to play the piano. I play the piano, and was glad that he wanted to play too. But then he stopped practicing and ultimately quit, and I felt badly. A short time thereafter he informed me that he had decided that he wanted to play the trumpet. I reacted very negatively, pointing out to him that he had already quit the piano and probably would quit the trumpet too.

I then found myself wondering why I had been so harsh. How could I have said such a thing? But then I quickly understood it. If someone else's child wanted to play the trumpet, that was fine. But I couldn't imagine any Sternberg child playing the trumpet. It did not fit my ideal image of a Sternberg child. I realized I was being narrow-minded and doing exactly the opposite of what I had told everyone else to do. It's one thing to talk the talk, another to walk the walk. I backpedaled, and Seth started playing the trumpet.

Eventually, he did, in fact, quit the trumpet. Finding the right thing is frustrating work! But Seth eventually did find the right thing. He went into business, working for IBM in acquisitions and divestitures of companies. Is it what I would have wanted for him? Doesn't matter! The important thing is that he found what is right for him. Find what is right for you, and let others find what is right for them.

❧ Lesson 21 ❧

Create Opportunities and Take Advantage of Them When They Arise

S OME YEARS AGO I realized that I felt that I was in a rut. I felt as though my research was moving in a direction different from that of my department, and I was thinking that it was time for a change. I had an offer from another university, and was considering leaving Yale.

At the same time, my group was in a particularly favorable position. We had just gotten a couple of large grants, and so were at an especially good time for initiating new research projects. I talked to a high-level administrator at the university that had offered me a job about the possibility of my starting a center on abilities, but somehow the idea had not quite clicked with him. He was not oppositional, but did not seem to understand exactly what I wanted. Maybe that was because I was not sure of exactly what I wanted. I then spoke to some high-level administrators at my home institution, and they offered to give me space in another building, as my group had outgrown the space I had in the psychology department. We had a choice of buildings, and I immediately picked an old historical house at the north end of the campus.

So began the PACE Center at Yale. Today it is a group of about 30 individuals—three times the size of the group when we were housed in the psychology department—and we have people from all over the world and in a variety of different disciplines. It is a wonderful group of people and a wonderful environment. I don't know whether it will last forever—probably not. But it has totally changed my "fit" with the environment I'm in.

Basically, I did what I found one must do throughout one's entire career: Create opportunities. No one came to me and suggested I start a center. I saw a possibility, and with the collaboration of many invaluable colleagues, realized it. At any point in your career, you can create opportunities or wait for opportunities to come to you. I find that opportunities rarely come to you, although they sometimes do. The name of the game is to create opportunities, rather than waiting for them magically to appear.

Although one often must create opportunities, there are times when, almost out of nowhere, opportunities do arise. Some people take them; others let them go. The important thing is, if they are the right opportunities, to take them when they arise.

Some years ago, I received a phone call out of the blue asking me whether I would be interested in formulating a program for helping Venezuelan school children to develop their intellectual skills. I knew virtually nothing about Venezuela, did not speak a word of Spanish, and had little idea of how in the world I or anyone else could create a successful program to improve intellectual skills. But I recognized I was getting an opportunity that I probably would get only one time in my career. I grabbed it. I learned about Venezuela and its new Ministry for the Development of Intelligence, I learned Spanish (which I now speak fluently), and I thought long and hard about how to create a program to develop intellectual skills.

Many good things came out of my accepting the offer. I got to visit Venezuela several times and learn about the culture. I learned a new language (when I was in my early 30s), and have had many opportunities to use it over the course of my life. I created the *Intelligence Applied* program

(Sternberg, 1986). And I made many new friends. Things did not end as well as they might have. The government that offered me and others the chance to develop programs lost in the next election, and the programs were quickly dismantled. Indeed, the opposing party ran under a platform of making fun of the programs and saying that they were just a big waste of money. As a result of the election loss, I never got to evaluate that particular program. But I'm glad I took the opportunity when it arose, and would not have given it up for anything.

I have been editor of two journals of the APA. Each time I became editor, I tried to make substantive and meaningful changes in the journal. Each time I was president of an APA division, I tried to do something that would leave a lasting impact on the division. I may or may not have succeeded. But I did not want to let opportunities for meaningful change go by the wayside. Some people take offices for little more than what appears to be the purpose of putting the offices on their vitas. In one particularly egregious case, a colleague I know became president of an APA division, and simply disappeared. No one could get in touch with him. He apparently cared about getting the office, not about doing anything with it. The past-president essentially had to run the division for that year. Most people are not so crassly opportunistic. But people who blow opportunities often do it not just for themselves, but for others, as was the case for the individual who ran for the division presidency, won, and then proceeded to do nothing. The division deserved better, and so, perhaps, did the individual. After this, few people in the division wanted to have anything to do with him.

Many opportunities have come up during the course of my career: the opportunity to edit journals, the opportunity to be president of APA divisions, the opportunity to serve on various committees doing what I believed to be important work. In almost anyone's life, good opportunities come from time to time. Don't let them go!

One of the best ways to create opportunities is to surround yourself with smart, eager, enthusiastic people. At various times in your life, you may have the choice between being with people who are great at what they do or with people who are not so great. The better opportunities are almost always with the people who are great. You have more to learn from them than from people who are not as expert as you. In the short run, surrounding yourself with mediocre people may raise your self-esteem. But in the long run, you will lose opportunities to grow that only great colleagues can provide.

❧ Lesson 22 ❧

Remember That You Can Go Very Far on Reflective Hard Work

MY GRADUATE ADVISOR, Gordon Bower, used to say that what matters in a career is "throughput," how much you get done. There are many ways to increase your throughput, but perhaps there is no substitute for hard work.

A successful academic career does not come easily. Virtually everyone I know who is successful in academia has worked very hard. They may not show that they work hard, and they may even hide it. But they work hard, nevertheless. It does not matter whether they are the sharpest knife in the drawer, or one of the blunter ones: Hard work is almost a sine qua non for success.

You want not only to work hard, but also, to work smart. You need to think carefully about where you invest your resources. There will be many demands on your time. If you are going to work hard, then make sure you work hard on those things that are meaningful to you and will get you where you want to go.

Ericsson (1996) has argued that the not-so-secret secret of becoming an expert is deliberate practice—working hard at a task in a focused, deliberative, and reflective way. You become an expert writer by writing a lot, and by working to improve your writing while you are doing it. You become an expert teacher by teaching a lot, and by asking yourself how you can improve your teaching. If you want to become an expert at whatever you do, work hard at it, and continually ask yourself how you can get better.

I take weekly cello lessons from a master cello teacher, Ole Akahoshi, a member of the faculty at the Yale School of Music. A point he repeatedly makes is that what matters is not just how hard you practice, but how smart you practice. You have to listen to yourself, and ask yourself how you can make your music sound better. Just playing music over and over again does not make you play it better. Indeed, if you do not pay attention to what you are doing, you may end up just reinforcing your old mistakes. It is the same with work in psychology. You need to work hard, but always ask yourself how you can improve at what you are doing.

❧ Lesson 23 ❧

Balance Long-Term With Short-Term Goals

O NE OF THE PROBLEMS you face when you are starting out a career is how to balance the long-term with the short-term. On the one hand, long-term projects are often those that have the potential to make the most difference to a field. On the other hand, promotion and tenure decisions come upon one quickly, and if one does not have anything to show on one's vita, one can end up being in serious trouble.

I decided early in my career to use an "asset-allocation" plan. I would do some long-term projects that I was particularly interested in, at the same time that I would do some things that were shorter-term so that, in the short run, I would not be stuck without anything to show for my time as a faculty member. That strategy generally has served me well during my career.

I have seen other faculty members (and corporation executives, and many others!) go entirely for the short-term. I believe that such a mentality is mistaken. One may end up with more to show in the short run, but make little of a lasting contribution in the long run. One assistant professor in my department was publishing away in his early years, and even getting the articles into very good journals. But the projects were short-term, bite-sized projects, and they have been little cited. In the short-term, he accumulated many publications and a long vita. In the long-term, the work seems to have had little impact. You need to think both for the short- and the long-terms. You cannot ignore the short-term, because often you have things you need to accomplish and do not have much time in which to accomplish them. But you cannot ignore the long-term, because the long-term things are likely to make the most difference.

❧ Lesson 24 ❧

When You Make a Professional Commitment, Honor It if at All Possible

I ENJOY EDITING, and have edited many books, often in collaboration with students and other colleagues. Each edited book I undertake requires a set of authors to contribute chapters. There are some people whom I would like to ask to write but whom I do not ask because they have proven themselves to be unreliable. They say they will write, and then cop out, often at the last moment. In doing so, they show themselves not only to be unreliable, but to be lacking in consideration of others, because all authors in the book are affected if one person pulls out.

It is extremely important to meet the professional commitments you make. If you are not sure if you can meet a commitment, do not make it. If you make it, then do your best to meet it. If you absolutely cannot, then try to work out something with the person, persons, or organizations to whom you have committed yourself. Perhaps you can find someone else of equal standing to do what you said you would do; or perhaps you can work out a time schedule so that you will do what you said you would do, only a bit later. Remember, you may have good excuses, but the chances are that those to whom you have committed have heard these excuses, and many others like them, before.

I travel too darn much. I keep trying to cut back my travel schedule, but somehow it always ends up being onerous.

Sometimes a planned trip sounds really good at the time I make the plans, but then when the time rolls around for the trip, it no longer sounds so great. Sometimes what I see are long lines and irritating security procedures at airports, time lost listening to talks in which I am not terribly interested, meetings with people whom I do not always have any great desire to meet. But if I have made the commitment, I make every effort to keep it. It is a matter of respect for those to whom I have made the commitment, but also respect for myself. I do not want to view myself as someone who says one thing and does another. I've done it at times, but always felt pretty lousy about myself afterwards.

The most memorable example in my own life was when I agreed orally to sign a textbook contract with one company, and the acquisitions editor for the textbook (the person who contracts the book) and her boss agreed to come up to New Haven to have lunch with me the following week. After making this oral agreement by phone, an acquisitions editor for another company showed up at my home front door—literally—and persuaded me that I should sign with him. I did. He left with a signed contract. Monday morning I called the acquisitions editor who was planning to visit to tell her that I had signed with the other company, and I was truly sorry. But she and her boss had left for New Haven. I felt terrible. They arrived at my door. I gave them the bad news, and they left angry and feeling betrayed. Although my commitment had not been written, I had orally committed myself, and then backed out. I felt badly at the time and still do, more than 10 years later! My mistake was not in signing with the second publisher. It was in orally (and informally) committing myself to the first publisher, and then signing with the second. Although I was under great pressure to sign with one or the other publisher, I should have waited to commit myself, even orally, until I was absolutely sure that signing with the first publisher was the right thing to do. So: If you make a commitment, keep it!

❧ Lesson 25 ❧

Be Not a Saint, a Sinner, or a Sucker

WE SOMETIMES HEAR that the best path through life is a "middle way"—some hypothetical mean that guides you away from extremes. I believe that there is much to be said for finding such a middle way. Certainly this is true with regard to three traps psychologists sometimes fall into.

The first is the nobly motivated desire to be a "saint." In the course of your career, you receive interminable demands from many people for your time. In a typical day, for example, I get perhaps 100 to 150 e-mails. Some, but not many of them, are essential. Among the nonessential are some that are worth my time and many others that really are not. I often find the following:

1. Requests from high school, college, and sometimes graduate students for help on class papers, which usually are conveniently due the next day so they kindly request an immediate response. A typical e-mail of this kind lists 5 to 10 questions, all of which could be answered by reading even one of the many things I've written. But why bother to read anything when you can get a personal response from the author of the papers and save yourself the time of actually doing library research? I usually do write back to such individuals, but only to suggest they read one or two works that I will specify. I've always felt it highly unlikely they will read anything. More likely, they will try to find some other person who is willing to respond at length to their e-mail. In my view, such a response would place me in the "sucker," not the "saint," category. It is not my responsibility—or yours—to write student papers for the students who are supposed to be writing them. So I avoid the temptation to play saint, because I would not really be a saint if I helped them.

2. Requests from parents and other guardians for help with a personal problem they or their children are having. Often, I will get fairly lengthy descriptions of such problems from people I do not know. I sometimes will say something vague but then will suggest that the individual get professional help. Although you may feel like you are being a saint to respond at length to such queries, you actually are being either a sucker or, as likely, a sinner. First, if you are not licensed, you have no business giving anyone advice in your role as a psychologist. The only license I have is a driver's license, and that license, for better or worse, does not authorize me to give advice. Giving advice in your role as a psychologist if you are unlicensed is an ethically and legally questionable move. Second, no matter how much detail you receive in these e-mails (or letters or phone calls), it will almost never be enough for you to provide the kind of advice the person needs. The individual typically needs professional counseling, not a stab in the dark as to how you can help him or her. So you may think you are being helpful, but you perhaps really are not being helpful at all, and you may even be hurtful. Third, you may find yourself getting into what you thought was a one-round interchange, but what the correspondent sees as a continuing exchange of letters. More than once, I have been in a situation in which I answered one e-mail (even briefly), only to find that, for the correspondent, this was the beginning of a long round of letters, not just a single one. You therefore need to take care that you do not get sucked into an endless interchange. Again, what seems like sainthood is not.

3. Spam. Just delete it. Don't even consider replying, even to complain or to criticize the sender. Once you reply, you have identified yourself as an interested party, and you never know how many people your e-mail address will be sold to. Responding in any way is likely simply to generate more e-mail, not less.

There are other ways in which you can find yourself becoming a sucker when you thought you were being a saint.

Sometimes you will get requests for assistance from colleagues whom you do know. I typically respond favorably to such requests. I want to help out any colleague I can. But in the course of a career, one inevitably runs into people who do not know when to stop: Having received a favorable response to one request for help, they keep coming back, again and again, and soon you become sucked into being a source of help to someone who has managed to attach him or herself to you in a parasitic way. Often, one cannot tell in advance who these people are. And often, as well, the requests are so plaintive and the person so seemingly in need of further and further help that it is hard to say no. In these cases, painful though it can be, I believe you need to back off. I find relatively few such people, but enough to realize that, if I am not on my guard, I can begin to attract more and more of them, and to have less and less time both for my own work and for helping people who genuinely do need help.

There are some people in academia who truly seem like saints. They are always helping others at the expense of their own career. This is as bad a way to go as never helping other people. Many such people have difficulty getting pro- moted. Even if they do get promoted, they then have difficulty establishing a reputation for themselves. In the long run, they are less able to help others because they have not established their own careers. You need to look out for yourself, and for others, but neither to the exclusion of the other.

One way to look out for yourself is to realize that things are not always as they appear to be on the surface. One of the ways people can sucker themselves out is to believe that the "deep" structure of a place is the same as its "surface" structure. Consider a simple example. When I was hired by Yale, on the surface, I was hired to teach. My contractual obligation concerns appearing for a certain number of classes and teaching them successfully. But the main way I have been evaluated is not on the basis of what I nominally was hired to do. The main way I have been evaluated is for my research. The same would be true at most research-oriented universities: Teaching counts, but research counts more. So the surface structure of the culture concerns teaching, but the deep structure concerns and values research at least as much as, and probably more than, teaching. As Chris Argyris (1999) would say, sometimes the espoused theory is not the theory in use: What people say may not be what they do.

Consider a second example, which applies to individuals rather than organizations. I work in the field of intelligence, broadly defined. An important part of this field is the study of critical and creative thinking. Several investigators in my field specialize in one or both of these types of thinking. They will go from one venue to another, exhorting their audiences on the value of critical thinking. One of them, in particular, has many devotees of his way of teaching critical thinking. Some view him as something of a guru in this field. But here is the rub. When you use his methods, he insists that you use them in exactly the way he prescribes. If you diverge from the approved way of using his materials, then you are, in effect, kicked out of his inner circle. The irony of what he is doing seems to escape him. He encourages people, in the abstract, to think critically. But that encouragement seems not to apply to his devotees. Them he expects to follow him slavishly, or be excommunicated from his group. The theory he espouses is greatly at variance with the theory he uses.

In sum, it is important to be on the lookout both for what people say and what they do. Do not assume that the two are the same, because often, they do not correspond. If you want to know what is valued—what the tacit knowledge of an environment is—look for what really is rewarded, not just for what people say is rewarded. And then decide whether the reward system is for you. If it is not, make every effort to find another environment in which to function. You will be happier if you do.

❧ Lesson 26 ❧

Spread Yourself Neither Too Thin
nor Too Thick

BECAUSE THERE ARE so many demands on your time in an academic career, you will find more and more to do as your career advances further and further. You may find yourself with teaching obligations, administrative responsibilities, one or more research projects, writing articles and perhaps grant proposals, doing outside activities such as consulting, perhaps reviewing papers or grant proposals, informally advising students and colleagues, and so forth. And of course you have personal responsibilities as well! One of the joys of an academic career is the diversity it affords. In 27 years, I've never been bored because there is always so much to do. At the same time, I've seen many academics who fall prey to the trap of spreading themselves too thin. They try to do too much, and end up getting little done. I had one colleague who was involved in more projects than anyone could count, including the colleague, but who never seemed to finish any of them. The result was that her career did not go as she wished, and she antagonized people who expected work from her that never quite seemed to get done.

Spreading yourself too thin has several disadvantages. First, work you need to get done doesn't get done because you have too many other things to do. Second, you may disappoint others who expect work of you that you fail to complete in a timely manner. Third, you may give others the impression of being scattered or flighty. Finally, when it comes time to be evaluated, you may be disappointed with the result. Whereas you may feel like you've done a lot, you may find others criticizing your lack of productivity because so little got done.

I must admit that I have a tendency to spread myself too thin. No reason to keep it a secret, because anyone who knows me will say the same thing. So I try to build in safeguards. For example, I usually review articles I receive quickly. But if I am busy and they start to accumulate, I start turning down new reviews after I have three reviews waiting to be done.

The complementary mistake is to spread yourself too thick. There is a great temptation in academia to do very little, but do it to the extreme. For example, there are some people who will devote all their time to their research but neglect their teaching, or become so absorbed in teaching that they neglect their research. Then there are people who cannot say "no" and end up on every departmental or university committee imaginable.

Spreading yourself too thick, like spreading yourself too thin, has adverse consequences. When you come up for evaluation, it likely will seem like your evaluators are targeting you not for what you did, but for what you did not do. People often get by—at least in many university settings—if they make sure they cover all their bases, at least to some extent. Almost no one will expect you to be a super-teacher, a super-researcher, and a super-administrator too. But you probably will be expected to be at least adequate in all three, and perhaps to excel in one (or possibly two). If you leave one base totally uncovered, it is not only the base, but also, you, who will be exposed to potential grief.

The same principle that applies across areas of endeavor applies within an area of endeavor. For example, in teaching, you may be expected to be at least decent in different kinds of teaching (e.g., lectures, seminars, one-on-one mentoring). If you do at least a reasonable job of all three, then you can probably afford to be better in one (e.g., seminars) and not as good in the others. But again, it pays to have your bases covered. Similarly, in research, you need to pay attention to many things—the theoretical background, who the participants are and how many of them you have, what materials you use and how well they sample the domain they are supposed to sample—and so on. Failing to pay attention to any one aspect of a study can result in the study's being rejected just because that one aspect was neglected.

In sum, spread yourself neither too thick nor too thin. Try to allocate your resources carefully. Find the right way to divide your time, and then stick with it.

❧ Lesson 27 ❧

Specialize, But Not to the Point of Losing the Forest for the Trees

PEOPLE HAVE DIFFERENT STYLES in their careers. Some like to move from one topic to the next, others to find one topic to dig into and then to stay with that topic indefinitely. In my experience, going to either extreme is a mistake.

If you very quickly move from one topic to another to another, you are likely to be viewed as flighty. When people in a given field are asked to evaluate you, they may think that you have done little because they know only or primarily your work in that field. Such a superficial approach to problems is generally devalued in the field of psychology. Departments are often reluctant to hire or retain people who are viewed as superficial.

Although the rewards of the field tend to be for depth, my own personal opinion is that some people carry "depth" too far. They start working on one problem and then never leave it. I think an analogy of research (and often, of teaching and administrative work) to a goldmine can be apt. Usually, when you first start mining gold from a given mine, you do not find the richest veins. Eventually, by careful planning and follow-through, you do find these richest veins. Then, after a point, the mine starts to become exhausted and the gold it has to yield more and more elusive. Part of any career is knowing when to move on.

It is for this reason that, for example, terms as editor of a journal tend to be fixed, as do terms as chair of a psychology department. After a while, new blood is needed. Journals in which the same person stays as editor for an indefinite term show, in my opinion, signs of exhaustion. And younger people are deprived of a chance to contribute their editorial skills. Similarly, research areas tend to yield only so much gold. As a research area becomes more and more mature, the amount of interesting new information per article in that area often starts to decrease. Research areas are not abandoned, for the most part, because all the questions in them are answered. On the contrary, few questions in psychology are ever answered for good! Rather, they are abandoned because they become boring. But there are, in any field, people who seem incapable of being bored, and they often find themselves doing more and more that interests other people less and less. It therefore is important to know when to move on.

So I believe it is worthwhile to find a middle ground between overspecialization, where you work on just one problem or in just one narrow area, and underspecialization, in which you are a jack of all trades but a master of none. You will have the most satisfying career, I believe, if you are focused, but versatile and willing to try out new things.

❦ Lesson 28 ❦

If You Do It Well, You'll Most Likely Do It Again

YEARS AGO, I ACCEPTED A JOB as associate editor of a journal, *Child Development*. I thought I did a reasonable job of it. Perhaps I did, because soon thereafter I was asked to be associate editor of a second journal (*Intelligence*). Then I became editor of a journal (*Psychological Bulletin*) and after that of still another journal (*The APA Review of Books: Contemporary Psychology*). Now my whole career does not follow this pattern. About 10 years ago, I was on a university committee for choosing assistant professors to win special university fellowships in the social sciences. I showed up for what I thought was the meeting and was surprised to see that I did not know anyone at the meeting. The reason was that I was at the wrong meeting: My committee had met the week before, and I had been a no-show. I learned my lesson, and now double-check dates and times of meetings.

Tom Carew, formerly chair of the Department of Psychology at Yale, used to tell me, "No good deed goes unpunished." What he meant was that if the university (or anyone else) finds out that you do something particularly well, you can expect to be asked to do it again and again. It therefore behooves you to ask yourself, in taking on a new responsibility, not only what the responsibility is, but where it is likely to lead you.

In sum, if there is a particular kind of task you like, accept opportunities to do it: You will probably be asked to do it more, if you do a reasonably good job. But if there is a kind of task you do not like to do, beware. If you do it and

71

do a good job, you may end up doing it again and again. When Wendell Garner came to Yale as a faculty member, he came partly because he was sick and tired of being an administrator at Johns Hopkins, and wanted to do something different, namely, be just a regular faculty member. Within a short amount of time, he was department chair, and shortly thereafter, he was selected as dean of the graduate school. He had the misfortune of being good at something he did not particularly like to do, and at something many others do not do well. He also had trouble saying no, so he ended up doing administration when he probably would have rather done his research full-time.

❧ Lesson 29 ❧

Believe in Yourself and Yours

IN ANY CAREER THERE COME TIMES when you feel that many people, perhaps most people, do not believe in you. It may be that you are going through a period of having conflict with others; or that you have an idea that you really like but no one else seems to; or that you get a string of articles or grant proposals turned down, or perhaps both; or it may be that you simply are chronically insecure. But such times should be expected in every career.

I've had many such periods. Right now, I just came out of a string of grant proposals turned down. I find myself wondering whether perhaps my research program is "washed up," or, at least, perceived that way. Then, finally, I got a proposal funded, and at a high level. Other times, I've had one article after another rejected. When I was being considered for tenure, I went through a very hard time (as do many people), and then someone very close to me at the time but outside the field of psychology commented that maybe I wasn't so hot after all—after all, this person commented, he had only my word that my work was any good. Years later, this same individual commented that he had heard from someone in the field that I had retreated into obscurity, and I found myself agreeing. Bad idea! I never should have agreed with him. No matter how bad things get, it is extremely important never to lose confidence in yourself—to come to believe that you really can't do much of anything. (Strictly speaking, I refer here to loss of what sometimes is called "self-efficacy," not "self-esteem." Self-efficacy refers to your belief that you can accomplish the tasks you need to accomplish, whereas self-esteem refers to a more generalized high opinion of oneself

73

that is not necessarily linked to task performance.) The problem is that once you lose your belief in yourself, you have nothing to keep you going.

For some reason, much, and I suspect, most of the feedback people get in the field of psychology is negative. Acceptance rates of articles by journals are very low, which means that most people are going to get their articles turned down most of the time. Grant funding is very limited, and in the typical grants competition, many more people are turned down than are funded. Students are often very demanding, and those who are most likely to come to you with negative comments are often likely to be among the dissatisfied.

Dean Simonton (1997) has found that, as creative individuals grow older, they become less and less productive. There may be several reasons for deceasing productivity. They may be busy in managerial or committee roles; they may be spending more time on teaching; they may be intellectually or even physically exhausted. But one thing I see commonly is that they become scared. They learn that eminence is no protector against critical feedback, and they may stop producing because they have tenure and do not need to produce, and because often it is even more embarrassing to receive negative reviews of your work later in your career than it is to receive them earlier. So they may become self-protective, and give up. Why expose themselves to ridicule?

Dean Simonton is a premier researcher in the field of creativity. He perhaps studies creativity in part because of his own experiences. He has described to me (personal communication, February 9, 2000) how, when he was in graduate school, he was roundly criticized by some of his professors for the kind of historiometric work (i.e., quantitative studies based on historical documents and records) he was starting to do in his studies of creativity. One professor told Simonton that he never would achieve even one publication in a first-line journal. Had Simonton lost faith in himself, he never would have continued with the research that has landed him numerous publications in first-line journals and made him one of the most widely cited psychologists in the field of creativity, or in any field.

Often, once you start losing confidence in yourself, it is difficult to turn back because you create a self-fulfilling prophecy. If you do not believe in yourself, you often convey that attitude to others, who may stop believing in you as well. You often act in ways that do not inspire confidence in others. So you become a loser not because you originally were, but because you thought you were.

Some years ago, I was invited to give a talk in a rather rough—and indeed, some might say, dangerous—section of a large city. I was rather worried about the whole prospect, especially because the talk was to be given at night, and by the time I was done and left, it would be dark. I was driving, and worried about getting lost. What especially worried me is that I felt I had a lousy sense of direction, and if anyone would get lost, it would be me.

I drove to the school where I was to give the talk, carefully following the complex directions I had been given and paying attention to all the numerous twists and turns in the roads. I got to the school without much trouble. At the end of the talk, I had to return along the reverse of the route I had taken to get to the school. I could no longer read the directions because it was too dark. What would happen if I got lost?

I left the talk, carefully paid attention to the streets, and got out of the raunchy section of town without a hitch. I then realized something about myself. I had always told myself I lack a sense of direction. As a result, when people would give me directions, I often would not pay much attention to them, figuring that I would get lost anyway. Then I did get lost, not because I could not follow directions, but because I had not paid attention. But my getting lost further convinced me that

I lacked a sense of direction, and so I created a self-fulfilling prophecy for myself. I "knew" I was incompetent. So I did not try to do the tasks. Then I failed on the tasks. And my failure reinforced my sense of incompetence. The lesson I learned is that by telling ourselves we cannot do things, we often become unable to do them. One of the most important things you can have is a sense of self-efficacy—a sense that you can do what you set out to do. When we hire people at the PACE Center, that sense is the first thing we look for. Telling yourself you can do something does not guarantee you can do it. But telling yourself you can't do it almost certainly guarantees that you won't, because you will not even try. It is thus important not to give up on yourself.

❦ Lesson 30 ❦

Remember That There Is Always Room To Grow

WHEN I WAS A GRADUATE STUDENT, Bill Estes, then a professor at Harvard, gave a colloquium at Stanford. He started it off by noting that he himself had funded the research he was going to discuss that day. People gasped. How could such a famous and well-regarded scientist fail to obtain funding for his work? Estes explained that, previously, he had had no trouble gaining funding to study memory-based phenomena. But then, he submitted to his funding agency a proposal to study perception rather than the usual proposal to study memory. The reaction of the grant panel was that if Estes wanted to study memory, the field in which he had established his reputation, that decision was fine. But they were unwilling to fund him to study perception. They said that they did not know whether he could succeed in an entirely different field. Estes therefore funded himself, succeeded, and later gained fame—as well as funding—in his new area of endeavor. Only through his willingness to grow and escape pigeonholing was he able to turn to a whole new field of creative endeavor.

There will be many attempts to pigeonhole you. Some attempts other people will make. But other attempts you yourself will make. You tell yourself that you can do certain things but not others. Bill Estes was willing to go beyond such pigeonholing, and relatively late in his career, start a new area of research. He could do it. So can you.

❧ Lesson 31 ❧

Don't Take Yourself Too Seriously

WHEN I WAS YOUNGER, I was determined never to become dead wood in my department. I even asked my students, if I ever did become dead wood, to throw me out my office window. I did not want to become an embarrassment to others, but most of all, to myself.

I remember going through an exercise of trying to figure out what the faculty members whom I considered to be dead wood had in common. I finally figured it out. I decided that what they had in common was that they all took themselves very, very seriously. They thought that they had found "truth" somewhere along the line, and they therefore stopped growing. Such people become ponderous, overly serious, and just downright boring. They are mentally moribund, but seem to be the only ones not to know it. Often, unfortunately, they can be in positions of power, and make life miserable for everyone, not just for themselves. You may not be able to change them. But you can make yourself who you want to be. Don't become a crashing bore. Realize that it is important to maintain a sense of humor, most of all, about yourself.

❧ Lesson 32 ❧

Learn When It Is Time To Make Gracious Exits

JUST AS IT IS IMPORTANT in life to know when to enter a situation, so also is it important to learn when to leave. There are many situations where gracious exits are important.

Say you are in a question or discussion session. Say you make a point. Then someone else responds. Then you respond. Then they respond. Such exchanges can go on well beyond the point at which anyone is learning anything if neither party to the exchange is able to leave well enough alone. There comes a point when it is time to stop such exchanges.

I remember an exchange in a journal between scholars that I observed when I was young. Professor X wrote an article. Professor Y responded. Professor X responded to Professor Y's response. Then Professor Y responded to Professor X's response. I think it would have gone on forever had not the journal editor declared the exchange over. By that point, I doubt anyone besides the two antagonists still was interested in the exchange.

One of the most painful kinds of examples of "no exit" is the blabbermouth in a symposium who seems to believe that he or she has a direct pipeline to God, and that the audience will be deprived of divine truth unless he or she keeps talking. Meanwhile, others who follow that person in the symposium are stewing in their chairs, watching their time evaporate. It has happened to me many times. A motormouth gets up and seems unable to shut up. Having something worthwhile to say seems to be irrelevant. The person just loves the sound of his or her own voice, and cannot seem to stop listening to it. It is the responsibility of symposium moderators to shut such people up, but often they fail to do their job, to everyone's disappointment—except the motormouth's.

Sometimes you need to make a gracious exit after you give a talk. A question-and-answer period starts. Then you discover, to your horror, that there is no moderator to stop it, or that the moderator is unwilling to stop it. Sometimes you just have to say "I'd be glad to answer one more question," because if you don't, possibly no one else will take responsibility for ending the session.

Perhaps the most important decision about a gracious exit comes at the end of a career. When do you "call it a day" and decide to retire? I never thought much about this issue when I was younger, but have thought about it more and more as I have grown older. On the one hand, I've seen some individuals retire when they still seemed to have a lot to contribute. On the other hand, I've seen individuals go on, and embarrass themselves and others. They are over the hill, and usually everyone knows it except them. I personally believe it is important to exit with your dignity intact. It probably behooves us all to seek sincere advice from others because it may be so difficult for us to know when the time has come to move on.

❧ Lesson 33 ❧

Realize That Knowledge Is a Double-Edged Sword

SOME YEARS AGO, I was visiting a very famous psychologist who lives abroad. As part of the tour he had planned for me, he invited me to visit the local zoo. We went past the cages of the primates, who were, at the time, engaged in what euphemistically could be called unexpected sexual behavior. I, of course, averted my eyes. However, my host did not do the same. After observing the primates for a short amount of time, he began to speak. I was astounded to hear him analyze the sexual behavior of the primates in terms of his theory of intelligence. It was as though he had come to see almost everything in terms of his theory of intelligence, applying the theory way beyond where it properly applied. In effect, his expertise had caused him to experience a kind of tunnel vision—a narrowing of his scope. I realized at that time, as I have many times since, how knowledge and expertise can be a double-edged sword.

On the one hand, one cannot be creative without knowledge. Quite simply, one cannot go beyond the existing state of knowledge if one does not know what that state is. Many students have ideas that are creative with respect to themselves, but not with respect to the field because others have had the same ideas before. Those with a greater knowledge base can be creative in ways that those who are still learning about the basics of the field cannot be.

At the same time, those who have an expert level of knowledge can experience tunnel vision, narrow thinking, and entrenchment. Experts can become so stuck in a way of

81

thinking that they become unable to extricate themselves from it. Such narrowing does not just happen to others. It happens to everyone, myself included. For example, at one point in my career, every theory I proposed seemed to have three parts. (Of course, there were *three* good reasons for this . . . .) At that point, I was "stuck on threes." Learning must be a lifelong process, not one that terminates when a person achieves some measure of recognition. When a person believes that he or she knows everything there is to know, he or she is unlikely to ever show truly meaningful creativity again.

The upshot is that I tell my students that the teaching–learning process is a two-way process. I have as much to learn from my students as they have to learn from me. I have knowledge they do not have, but they have flexibility I do not have—precisely because they do not know as much as I do. By learning from, as well as teaching to, one's students, one opens up channels for creativity that otherwise would remain closed.

If a student has an idea that I don't like, I will tell him or her. But I will also acknowledge that it's only my opinion, and I may be wrong. I will encourage the student to present at one of our two weekly meetings, and as often as not, others will see value I do not see. We all can become imprisoned by our own expertise. But we also can free ourselves of this prison if only we choose to do so.

❦ Lesson 34 ❦

Give Students and Colleagues Direction but Allow Them the Freedom To Find Themselves

WHETHER YOU ARE a colleague or a mentor, you may or may not have a style or set of styles that matches the styles of the people you work with. But it is important to try to adapt yourself so that you can work with a wide variety of people. In the course of a career, you will be working in various capacities with thousands of people. Many of the things you work on will be team efforts in which collaboration is the name of the game. If you cannot collaborate successfully, you find your endeavors do not have the success that you ideally would like to have.

In my own theory of mental self-government, I distinguish among several different thinking styles (Sternberg, 1997b). People do not simply have one style or another. Rather, they have a profile of styles that may vary across tasks or situations. But many people do show consistent patterns of preference. I mention here some but not all the styles in the theory of mental self-government. It is important to realize that styles are not fixed: One can modify one's styles through self-analysis and determination. One can achieve success with any set of styles: It is a matter of figuring out how to make one's styles work for oneself.

The first three styles refer to "functions" of mental self-government.

- *Legislative.* The legislative person likes to decide what to do, and when, where, and how to do it. This is the kind of person who often likes to give rather than receive direction.

- *Executive.* The executive person prefers to be given fairly explicit guidelines within which to work and often prefers more to less structured tasks. This is the kind of person who often prefers to receive rather than give direction, or at least to receive direction and then pass it along to others.

Legislative and executive people often work well together. The legislative person likes to give direction to the executive person, and the executive person likes to receive direction from the legislative person. There are two caveats, however. The first is that when the relationship becomes too asymmetrical, the legislative person may become bored or frustrated with the executive person, and the executive person may become resentful of the legislative person. The second is that the two people will work well together, assuming that the executive person accepts the program of the legislative person, and the legislative person accepts the manner of working of the executive person. Two legislative people can be tremendously stimulating to one another, because they are both "ideas" people, but they may clash if their ideas are different or if each competes to have his or her ideas implemented. Moreover, they may find that they have trouble getting things done. Each may feel that it is the other's responsibility actually to implement the ideas. Two executive people can get along very well if they feel that they are "on the same page," that is, following the same general program of action. They may do so in their work, or in their personal lives or elsewhere. But they tend to look for direction to the outside, and if the direction they follow is misguided, they may be in serious trouble.

- *Judicial.* The judicial person likes to judge people and products. This individual tends to be judgmental in relations with others, and to use his or her judgments to determine how to behave toward others.

Judicial people can work well with legislative people if they are constructively rather than destructively critical of the legislative people's ideas. They can work well with executive people if they are constructively critical of the way the executive people get things done. They can work well with each other so long as their criticism is directed outside the relationship. If they turn their criticism inward—toward each other—they can be in serious trouble.

The next four styles pertain to structures of mental self-government.

- *Monarchic.* Monarchic people tend to be single-minded. They are directed toward a single goal and tend to be impatient with people or things that get in the way of their achieving that goal.

Monarchic people can be very helpful when there is a goal to be reached and there are many potential distractions or obstacles to reaching that goal. They tend to blaze through distractions and obstacles and thereby to accomplish, often within a very reasonable time frame, tasks that other people may take longer to get done, or never get done at all. At the same time, monarchic people can be difficult to work with if there are multiple and even competing goals on the agenda. The monarchic person may be so directed by his or her single preferred goal that progress toward other potentially important goals is impeded.

- *Hierarchic.* The hierarchic person likes to engage in multiple activities within a single time frame, and to set priorities for accomplishing the different activities.

The hierarchic person is usually an easy one to work with, so long as your priorities match those of the hierarchic individual.

- *Oligarchic.* The oligarchic person also likes to engage in multiple activities within a single time frame, but does not like to set priorities.

Oligarchic people often are difficult to work with, because they are as likely to be spending their time on projects that are not very important as on projects that are important. Moreover, they sometimes tend to misallocate time, spending more time on unimportant projects and less time on important projects than is desirable. Sometimes it is helpful to them simply to give them priorities so that they can allocate their resources in a more effective manner.

- *Anarchic.* Anarchic people eschew particular systems for doing things. They tend to be scattered in their approach and often to be hard to understand.

Anarchic people can be extremely difficult to work with because they seem at times to be "all over the place." Their conversations often change rapidly from one topic to another and the projects they work on also may change very rapidly. At the same time, they often have an unusual potential for creativity because they are willing to grab ideas and information from disparate and often seemingly irrelevant sources. The question becomes one of whether they are able to channel their creative potential effectively.

The next two styles are orientations of mental self-government.

- *Internal.* The internal individual is someone who prefers to work by him or herself. Internal people tend to be introverted and to work best when left to their own devices.

Internal people risk losing out on opportunities to profit from interactions with other people. But an advantage they have is that if, at a given time, their colleagues are not ones from whom they particularly can profit or with whom they get along particularly well, they can continue to work relatively effectively and with only relatively minor disruption.

- *External.* The external individual prefers to work with others and to engage in collaborative enterprises. External people tend to be extroverted and to work best in collaborations.

Externals have the pattern opposite to that of internals. They profit particularly well when they have strong colleagues, but may be at something of a loss when they do not.

It is important in evaluating people to beware of falling into the trap of evaluating them not for their quality or the quality of what they do, but rather, for their match to your styles of thinking. We have found that teachers tend to evaluate more highly students whose styles of thinking match their own (see Sternberg, 1997b; Sternberg & Grigorenko, 1995). Thus, they are valuing the students not for the quality of their work, exactly, but for the extent to which the students and their work match the teachers' ways of seeing and doing things. You need to recognize that styles are not better or worse, just different. If you open yourself to valuing people for what they have to contribute, not just for their similarity to you, everyone will be better off. So understand your own styles, and how they affect your work and your collaborations with other people.

❧ Lesson 35 ❧

It Is More Important, Ultimately, To Be Wise Than Just To Be Smart

THERE ARE MANY smart people in the field who are not wise. But the people who serve as the best mentors and ultimately, I believe, who contribute the most to the field, are people who are wise as well as smart. When I speak of wisdom I refer to the application of intelligence and experience as mediated by values toward the achievement of a common good through a balance among your own, others', and institutional interests, over the short and long terms (Sternberg, 1998a, 2001).

Thus, wisdom is not just about maximizing one's own or someone else's self-interest, but about balancing off various self-interests (intrapersonal) with the interests of others (interpersonal) and of other aspects of the context in which one lives (extrapersonal), such as one's city or country or environment or even God.

An implication of this view is that wisdom goes beyond just street smarts, or practical intelligence. When one applies practical intelligence, one may deliberately seek outcomes that are good for oneself and bad for others. In wisdom, one certainly may seek good ends for oneself, but one also seeks common good outcomes for others. If one's motivations are to maximize certain people's interests and minimize other people's, wisdom is not involved. In wisdom, one seeks a common good, realizing that this common good may be better for some than for others. An evil genius may be academically intelligent; he may be practically intelligent; but he or she cannot be wise.

Problems requiring wisdom always involve at least some element of each of intrapersonal, interpersonal, and extrapersonal interests. For example, one might decide that it is wise to take a particular teaching position, a decision that seemingly involves only one person. But many people are typically affected by an individual's decision to take a job—significant others, children, perhaps parents and friends. And the decision always has to be made in the context of the whole range of available options.

What kinds of considerations might be included under each of the three kinds of interests? Intrapersonal interests might include the desire to enhance one's popularity or prestige, to make more money, to learn more, to increase one's spiritual well-being, to increase one's power, and so forth. Interpersonal interests might be quite similar, except as they apply to other people rather than oneself. Extrapersonal interests might include contributing to the welfare of one's school, helping one's community, contributing to the well-being of one's country, or serving God, and so forth. Different people balance these interests in different ways. At one extreme, a malevolent dictator might emphasize his or her own personal power and wealth; at the other extreme, a saint might emphasize only serving others and God.

Wisdom involves a balancing not only of the three kinds of interests, but also of three possible courses of action in response to this balancing: adaptation of oneself or others to existing environments; shaping of environments to render them more compatible with oneself or others; and selection of new environments. In adaptation, the individual tries to find ways to conform to the existing environment that forms his or her context. Sometimes adaptation is the best course of action under a given set of circumstances. But typically one seeks a balance between adaptation and shaping, realizing that fit to an environment requires not only changing oneself, but changing the environment as well. If an individual finds it impossible or at least implausible to attain such a fit, he or she may decide to select a new environment altogether, leaving, for example, a job, a community, a marriage, or whatever.

It is easy to point to examples of people who are (or were) quite intelligent but, in key respects, unwise. Some are psychologists. A department chair who runs a department for his or her own benefit or the benefit of the area of psychology from which he or she comes is unwise. A researcher who fabricates data or a teacher who comes to class unprepared: Each is failing to take into account the interests of others.

I can find some examples of less than wise behavior in my own repertoire. When I was younger, I sometimes criticized opponents of my positions in a manner that I thought was clever, but also, that was snide. This way of criticizing them was unwise, because it did not convince them that I had a better way of seeing things than they did, but rather, just antagonized them further. Being snide or aggressive in one's critiques is an ineffective way of convincing people to see one's point of view.

But foolishness can be found at least as readily outside psychology as within. Bill Clinton comes to mind: He has a degree from Yale Law School and was a Rhodes Scholarship winner. In my opinion, he did some wonderful things during his administration; but he made something of a mess of his presidential administration in his choices of paramours and of people to pardon. Richard Nixon opened communication with China. But at the same time, he was as ardent in covering up the break-in at the Democratic Headquarters in Washington's Watergate Hotel as Clinton was in covering up his sexual liaisons. Both individuals illustrated how often it is not the act, but rather, the cover-up, that does one in. There are so many examples of this principle that it is worth keeping in mind (see below). Why are smart people sometimes so foolish? Keep reading!

❧ Lesson 36 ❧

Avoid the Five Major Pitfalls
of the Foolish

RADOVAN KARADZIC, wanted for war crimes committed in Bosnia, is, if anything, well-educated. He is a medical doctor, a psychiatrist, in fact. Unfortunately, he is not alone among war criminals in his attainment of impressive educational credentials: Many top-ranking Nazis were highly educated, possessing doctoral degrees of various kinds. Similarly, today's most frightening terrorist is not an uneducated young male yanked off the streets, but rather, a well-educated, carefully trained individual bent on destruction.

Traditional education, and the intellectual and academic skills it provides, furnish little protection against evil-doing or, for that matter, plain foolishness. The United States has had some very well-educated politicians and even presidents whose foolishness in their lives has cost them and their reputations dearly. The recent Enron, Global Crossing, and World-Com scandals have made clear that the shenanigans of the well-educated apply to business as well as politics, and those of us who reside in the groves of academe know that foolishness can be found there as well.

I recently have edited a book, *Why Smart People Can Be So Stupid* (Sternberg, 2002c), in which scholars who specialize in the study of human intelligence analyze why it is that smart people can do such stupid things. My own view is that smart and well-educated people often are particularly susceptible to five fallacies, precisely because they *are* so skilled:

91

1. The *"what-me-worry" fallacy,* named after an expression used by *Mad* magazine's Alfred E. Neuman, whereby they believe that they are so smart, whatever they do will work out all right;

2. The *egocentrism fallacy,* whereby they come to believe that the world revolves, or at least *should* revolve, around them. They then act in ways that benefit them, regardless of what the effects may be on other people;

3. The *omniscience fallacy,* whereby they come to believe that they know all there is to know, and therefore do not have to listen to the advice and counsel of others;

4. The *omnipotence fallacy,* whereby they come to believe that their brains and education somehow make them all-powerful; and

5. The *invulnerability fallacy,* whereby they come to believe that not only can they do what they want, but that others will never be clever enough to figure out what they have done or, even if others do figure it out, to get back at them.

The high and mighty often have spectacular rises, followed by spectacular falls, because they succumb to those fallacies. Numerous examples abound—in recent times, the Enron fiasco comes to mind. Some very smart people did some very foolish things. What *were* these people thinking when they did what they did? According to the present view, they were thinking something like that they were omniscient, omnipotent, and invulnerable, and they were thinking largely, or even entirely, of themselves as opposed to others.

It once was thought, and many people still believe, that intelligence and education are the answer, but they appear not to be. A variety of studies show that higher levels of education are associated with higher intelligence. But what do these advantages buy one?

Luis Alberto Machado, in the early 1980s the Minister for the Development of Intelligence in Venezuela and probably the first such minister in world history, believed that higher intelligence somehow would create better, more humane people. But does it?

Research by James Flynn (1999) has shown that, during the twentieth century, IQs increased by an average of about 9 points per generation (although one could not detect this increase simply from looking at the standardized test scores, because the tests were renormed every so often to bring the mean IQ back to 100). This increase was essentially worldwide, and was probably due in part to better education. But the twentieth century also saw historic levels of massacres and genocides, not just in Nazi-occupied Europe, but also in Bosnia, Rwanda, Burundi, Cambodia, Russia, and many other places. So whatever concomitants occur with increased intelligence, wisdom does not necessarily appear to be one of them. Indeed, focusing exclusively on the development of academic skills may take time away from activities that might help to develop wisdom. Academic skills are important, of course, but they are not all-important. As the example of Karadzic pointed out, some of the most highly intelligent and educated people use their skills cynically to foment hate and violence. We need to develop wisdom and also to avoid the four fallacies of foolishness that can ruin anyone's career.

One would like to believe that training in psychology would somehow prevent psychologists from being foolish. After all, their training is in understanding human nature. Perhaps such training does make them quicker to spot foolishness in others. But I've seen no evidence in my career that the training makes one iota of difference in terms of psychologists' own lives. Psychologists can compete with anyone for foolish acts.

❧ Lesson 37 ❧

When You Make Mistakes, Admit Them, Learn From Them, and Move On

EVERYONE MAKES MISTAKES. I do; you do; all the people you know about and care about do. Making mistakes is not in itself a source of variation among individuals, although certainly some people may make more than others. What is a source of variation is the extent to which people are willing to admit to their mistakes, learn from them, and move on. In our work on practical intelligence (e.g., Sternberg et al., 2000), we have found that the people who are the most successful often are those who admit to and learn from mistakes. They are not necessarily the people with the highest IQs. In general, I have found that people who are unable or unwilling to admit mistakes, and who react defensively to criticism, no matter how constructive it is, have a relatively poor prognosis for success in the field.

There are several problems with not admitting mistakes. One is that you are likely just to keep making the same mistakes. A second is that the mistakes you make that you do not admit to are likely to keep coming back to you. They never pass you by because you have not allowed yourself to put them behind you and move on. The third problem is that others are likely to think less of you.

In our center at Yale, people who have been unable to admit to mistakes have never worked out well. They have trouble getting their articles accepted because they ignore feedback from referees. They have trouble getting funded because, when they revise their grant proposals, the proposals look to reviewers pretty much like the earlier versions did.

And they have trouble working with other people because they keep making the same mistakes in their interactions with others.

One of the more serious cases I have seen of someone who could not admit to mistakes was that of a member of a psychology faculty who was exploitative of other people—students, schools in which she worked, even other faculty. The exploitation was rather blatant. Relationships for her were clearly defined by what was in them for her. She was unwise, in the sense that she pretty much considered only her own interests and not the interests of others or of the institution. Students complained and even school districts complained and she received detailed and repeated feedback. But her reaction was to blame the messenger bringing the bad news and to insist that there was an organized conspiracy against her. It never was clear who was behind the conspiracy or why they would have fomented it. But she never changed her views, was encouraged to leave, and eventually left. Exploiting others is always a mistake, and she seemed to be unable either to recognize this fact or to recognize her own tendency to engage in it. She made a mistake, and then made it again and again and again. Don't you do the same!

It is important in your career, not only to admit to your mistakes, but to take responsibility for them and for their consequences. People who take responsibility for their actions are more likely to learn from them and thus to improve the way they function. People who seek to blame others, or who simply are not willing to take responsibility for what they have done, do not quite recognize that they have a problem and hence are unable fully to address and ultimately to resolve it.

⚜ Lesson 38 ⚜

Don't Try To Please Everyone

YOU WILL COME upon times in your career when the opinions of particular other people are important to your future. Sometimes you will have to make an attempt to raise their opinion of you. In principle, there is nothing wrong with trying to make people happy. Where you go wrong is when you try to please everyone, or you are indiscriminate in whom you try to please. At times in my life, I have tried to please certain people and later regretted it. I regretted it because I realized that there simply are some people who will never be pleased with what I do, and that the more I try to please them, the less pleased I will end up being with myself. And I have decided it just is not worth selling myself out for their sake. I remember in particular trying to please a certain faculty member whom I had been told would oppose my bid for tenure. I realized that there was no way to please him. It didn't matter what I would do: He didn't like anything I did, and probably never would. So be it.

To give you a concrete example: In the field of intelligence—one of the main fields in which I work—there are fairly active disagreements over just what intelligence is. I am among those people who believe that intelligence has multiple facets that are distinct from each other. Other people in the field believe that intelligence is just one thing. I have, at times, tried to find compromise positions that would make some of these people—even the extreme ones—happy. I have found no compromise position that mollified them. And I have realized that there probably is none. We simply disagree. And it is OK to disagree.

❦ Lesson 39 ❦

Don't Sell Out

AS COLLEGE STUDENTS, we used to talk about "selling out." Going to college in the late 1960s and early 1970s, we considered selling oneself out to be the ultimate sin. Each of us wanted to be true to him- or herself. Few of us have been. And oddly enough, if one looks at who was true to the goals he or she set, it would have been hard to predict at the time which of us would be true to him or herself.

There are many different ways of selling out. You can go into a field just for the money, as did many of my friends. Almost all of them today are unhappy and just cannot wait until they retire. You can take positions in which you do not really believe, just to please others. Once you start on this path, you find yourself on a slippery slope. Eventually you may have trouble figuring out what you believe in, and others may as well.

The opportunities to sell out start early and continue. In my own case, I have had many opportunities. Some years ago, I found myself in disagreement with a superior in a particular situation over a whole number of issues. The superior was not very happy that I did not like the way he was doing things. Eventually, the superior must have gotten rather upset, because he said to me that "the train is leaving the station, and you can either get on it or not." The implication was that if I did "not get on the train," he would make my life rather unpleasant. So I had a choice: Get on his train or risk the consequences. I told him that I was not getting on. I have never regretted "sticking to my guns." I just did not want to get on his train; it was not the train for me.

Of course, I, like everyone else, make mistakes in my judgments. I have been involved in search committees that have made hires that later proved to be ill-considered. I have undertaken research projects with confidence, only to have them bomb out badly. I have trusted colleagues and employees whom I should not have trusted. But I have found that it is better to act upon what you believe rather than to sell out, even if you later come to the conclusion that your beliefs need to be modified. The challenges never end. Right now, I find myself disagreeing in some ways with the way the educational establishment is moving in the United States. There is more and more emphasis on very high-stakes testing, and testing that I believe to be of a narrow kind. It would be much easier for me simply to go along to get along. But I cannot do it. I am happy to work with people who disagree with me, but I find that I cannot fall silent or capitulate just for the sake of taking the easy way out. I hope you find the same.

❧ Lesson 40 ❧

Don't Bad-Mouth People Behind Their Backs

WHENEVER I HEAR someone bad-mouth someone else behind that person's back, it gets me very upset. First of all, it is not right. If you have something to say, you should be able to say it to the person's face. I try to say the same things to people about themselves that I say to others about them, and hope they will do the same for me. Second, bad-mouthing others invites them to do the same to you. Third, I realize that if someone I am talking to is bad-mouthing other people to me behind their backs, the chances are pretty good that the individual is doing the same thing to me behind my back. So when I hear someone bad-mouth others, I conclude that the individual is not trustworthy. There is no reason to expect the individual to treat anyone differently. Finally, if you expect that it will not get back to the people you bad-mouth, think again. It's a losing game, because sooner or later people discover the kind of person you are.

In fact, I do know someone who is a bad-mouther. He will appear to be good friends with people, and then, behind those people's backs, say things that I am sure he would never say to their faces. This individual made me very nervous, and indeed, I started to receive feedback that he was doing the same to me. Now I just try to avoid him. I also practice what I preach: I avoid saying anything of someone behind his or her back what I will not say to his or her face.

❧ Lesson 41 ❧

Be Generous With Your Time but Don't Let Others Rob You of It

EVERY DAY, I receive large amounts of e-mail from people
I do not know. Some are from people who want information that easily could be gotten from reading any of a number
of articles or books I have written or that are on my website.
I have colleagues who are willing to spend a great deal of
time answering such e-mails. I have decided that I am not.
Although I answer the e-mails—I view it as a professional
responsibility—I typically write back only briefly, suggesting
they consult the website or read a particular article and offering
to send it to them. I often then suggest that if, after reading
the article or website, they still have questions, they write
back. I realize that they may not read anything, and that I may
have missed an attempt to educate a member of the public
on some issue that I may really care about. But I just do not view
it as a good use of my time to answer individually questions that
I already have answered through my writings. I also receive
many e-mails from students who have questions for class
papers that they have to write. Again, I reply briefly, but am
not willing to answer the long lists of questions I sometimes
receive. To me, such demands are local, and not ones that
are worth much of my time. I am not saying others should
feel the same way. Rather, I am saying that we each must
decide what the important demands on our time are, and
plan accordingly.

❦ Lesson 42 ❦

Be Open and Be Straight

O N THE ONE HAND, it makes sense to talk to people in a kind and humane way. I strongly believe that there is no place for belittling or demeaning one's students, colleagues, or friends. At the same time, some people are afraid to say what they think. In my experience, the results are usually unfavorable. It is better to be open and straight.

I once had an assistant who seemed continually to be afraid to speak her mind. We would go through relatively long periods in which, no matter what I said to her, she would take it graciously and even meekly. And then, once a year or so, she would just explode. The explosion usually was set off by something minor, and would seem to be like an explosion of a powder keg. She had built up resentment in successive increments, and when the resentment reached some criterion level, the explosion would come.

There are several problems with this mode of relating. One is that problems that could have been solved weren't because she never shared with me what she perceived to be a problem. A second is that it is fundamentally not honest. She was thinking one thing and saying another. And a third problem is that, when the explosion did come, little was resolved. She would be so angry that any kind of meaningful discussion was very difficult to have. We both would have been much better off if, when she had something to say, she simply said it.

One form of not being straight is keeping inside you the issues you have with another person. Another form is being duplicitous. Years ago, I collaborated with someone on a research project. The project went well. Then, when we were discussing order of authorship (I thought she should be first author), the collaborator stunned me by saying that she thought Professor X should be first author. What was stunning was that I had not even known that Professor X had been involved in the project. So all of a sudden I was discovering a "silent partner." I rejected this request (which was posed almost as a demand) and talked to Professor X, who said he should not, in fact, be listed as a coauthor. I don't know whether it was my outrage or whether it was that he thought that the collaborator was off base. But this kind of duplicity almost certainly will spoil any relationship you have with anyone.

Being open with people can be painful at times, but in the long run it generally pays off. And I think people respect you more for it. Can I guarantee that there will never be people who will hold it against you? Of course not. There are people who will hold your honesty against you. But then the question is: Do you want to be like them, or to let them determine your behavior?

In being open with people, remember that there is always room for tact. You can say what you have to say in a nice way. But do them and yourself a favor: Say it.

❦ Lesson 43 ❦

Practice What You Preach

I LEARNED THIS LESSON from a set of professional colleagues with whom I attended a meeting on psychology and education in Hong Kong. The meeting I attended was on psychology and education, in general, but an important focus of it was on the value of letting people learn from mistakes (one of the lessons in this book). Too often, teachers inadvertently disempower students who make mistakes, with the result that students become afraid to make them. They thereby lose the opportunity to learn from their mistakes.

During one of the early talks at the meeting, a relatively well-known speaker was giving a lecture, and I was only half-listening because my mind was also engaged in thinking about something else. But I was attentive enough to catch the speaker in a major blooper—or so I thought. After he finished his talk, I raised my hand, prepared to deal the coup de grace to what to me seemed to be a pathetic line of argument. He called on me and I spoke my mind, forcefully but nicely. After I spoke, the room was so quiet that one could have heard a pin drop. I found myself wondering why the room was so quiet. At that point, one of my former advisors, who just happened to be in the audience, boomed out something like: "The reason no one is saying anything, Bob, is because he never said that. You totally misunderstood his point." I have rarely been so embarrassed. I just wished a trap door would open up in the floor and that I could fall deep within it. But no trap door opened up. And so I had to spend the rest of the meeting wearing what seemed to be an invisible but nonetheless notable badge of shame.

For the rest of the meeting, people treated me like a pariah. They looked at me and I felt they were thinking to themselves, "There goes the dummy!" If only it had been the last rather than the first day of the meeting, but no such luck.

Perhaps unfortunately for the conference organizers, they had invited me to present the final talk at the conference. I had prepared a set of remarks on the talks but when I started my final talk, I put aside my notes and made some extemporaneous remarks. I started off by saying that, at the beginning of the conference, I had put my foot in my mouth and made a damn fool of myself in the process. After all, I had made what turned out to be in all likelihood the most off-base remark of the entire conference. But I also pointed something else out.

A major theme of the conference was the importance of learning from one's mistakes. Everyone seemed to believe it was important and preached the importance of teaching it to students. But look what had happened to (poor old) me! I had made a mistake, and afterward, had been treated like something of a pariah. I said that the whole experience had been pretty painful, but that I was lucky in many ways, because I was in a conference far from home base, and eventually would leave it to go back home. Also, I was well into my 40s at the time and a full professor, so I had a series of decent accomplishments on which I could fall back. For me, it was not ego-shattering.

Suppose, though, that the same thing had happened to a younger person, one who was just starting out and did not have much of a track record yet. And suppose, worse, it happened on the individual's home base. How quickly would that person get over the mistake? And would not the person learn the very opposite of what the conference attendees were preaching, namely, the value of letting people learn from their mistakes? So here we were preaching, but not practicing what we preached.

Of course, I do not wish to imply that I always live up to this lesson either. I often tell students to think before they speak. The whole event never would have taken place if I had followed my own advice. We all need better to practice what we preach.

It is much easier to tell others to do something than it is to do it ourselves. For this reason, we need continually to be watching our own behavior to ensure that we do what we tell others to do. If we fail to do so, others quickly come to perceive us as empty windbags—as people who say one thing but do another. The result is that very soon they stop taking us seriously. If we want to be taken seriously, we need not only talk the talk, but also, walk the walk. Do not think that hypocrisy will go unnoticed. If you act hypocritically, you may or may not notice it. Other people almost certainly will.

❧ Lesson 44 ❧

Think Before You Speak

IN ALMOST ANY GROUP, there seems to be at least one individual who is the motor-mouth of the group—the person who always has something to say, and to say at length, regardless of whether it is worth saying or not. Such windbags often lose their credibility, because they are readily recognized as people who shoot off their mouths. But they can sometimes destroy themselves and others through their impulsivity.

I once consulted for an individual who was in a very high position in a company. At one point, the position above him became available, and he was one of the candidates for that position. He was very hopeful that he would get that position.

One day he received a telephone call from the CEO telling him that he did not, in fact, get the position. He was extremely distressed, and mouthed off to the CEO, telling him that it was a bad choice and that the CEO would regret the choice later on. In fact, the person who later had cause for regret was the motor-mouth. He not only did not get the promotion, within short order, he lost the job he had. It really pays to think before you speak!

In many groups, there seems to be a role that one person or another fills: The person who shoots his or her mouth off and seems to need to keep talking and talking. Such people are almost never the people called on to take critical roles in the group. They may have something to contribute. But they undermine their own credibility by their impulsive expatiations.

❧ Lesson 45 ❧

Realize That Networking Matters—
Up to a Point

I T IS SOMETIMES SAID that "it is not what you know, it's whom you know." That statement is, in my experience, false. What you know does matter. At the same time, whom you know matters, too. As APA president, I am involved directly or indirectly in many assignments of people to task forces, committees, and boards. There is no doubt that people who are known to the decision makers are more likely to be chosen. Similarly, in getting jobs, having some kind of personal contact or connection can make a difference in the result. Having genuine friendships, as mentioned earlier, is even better.

At the same time, there are people who try to use networking as a substitute for substance. In my experience, this strategy rarely pans out. It may work over the short term, but eventually people realize that you are an empty shell. And people often will resent that you attempt to substitute substance with show. Ideally, you will combine substance with a broad and deep network of associates.

I know one individual who seems to manage to be on every committee around. She seems to be the ultimate networker, and hence is asked to serve, again and again. But when I think about what the person has to show for having been on all these committees, it is hard to say, other than multiple lines on a vita. Networking is no substitute for substance. You want to develop a network not in place of substantive contributions, but rather, so that others can appreciate the substantive contributions you make. Networking is very important and needs to be developed in addition to rather than instead of substantive contributions.

❧ Lesson 46 ❧

Distinguish Between
More and Less Important Battles

IN DEPARTMENTAL MEETINGS, in APA Board meetings, and in almost any other interaction I have with anyone, discords sometimes arise. It is important to distinguish the battles from the wars. Some issues are worth fighting for and fighting for hard; others are not. It is important to learn early in your career which are which, and to act accordingly.

One of the most precious commodities in academia is space. I have been to many universities in which faculty members were slugging it out for space; I have not been to many where faculty members had more space than they could use (actually none, to be exact). Recently, I was engaged in a space battle. A few years ago, my colleagues and I acquired for our PACE Center a wonderful old house on the northern edge of the Yale campus. This historical house, built at the turn of the century, has actually had two U.S. presidents sleep in it (Taft and T. Roosevelt, who spent a night there ironing out differences they had) and has had a very distinguished history. The only problem is that we did not acquire all the rooms in the house for the PACE Center. Some of the rooms were then allocated to visitors in International Relations, and since then, have continued to be.

After protracted and difficult negotiations, we acquired more space from the university—across the street. So the plan was that our group would be split up and that the visiting faculty in International Relations would continue to occupy space in the house. We made numerous attempts this past spring to swap space and to do everything we could so that we could stay together. Every time we thought we had the space swap arranged, it fell through. Finally, we decided to occupy the space across the street. It was not our ideal. But it was clear that we had lost this battle, plain and simple. It just was not worth fighting anymore. We will be back, of course, and try to arrange the swap at some future time. But the battle simply was not important enough to continue. So we admitted defeat, and moved on. Sometimes in one's career, one has to decide which battles really matter and are worth pursuing to the end, and which ones aren't. We decided that this one wasn't.

❧ Lesson 47 ❧

Accept Losses Graciously

THE STORY OF the lost space battle is one of only hundreds of lost battles I could recount from the losing side of the tally sheet of my career. I have had articles turned down, grants denied, proposals to the department unceremoniously rejected, and so on. During the course of a career, you inevitably win some and lose some. People will judge you as much by the grace with which you handle losses as by the grace with which you accept wins.

There are plenty of sore losers in this business. They just cannot accept a loss. I am editor of a book-review journal, *The APA Review of Books: Contemporary Psychology*. The journal cannot review every book that is published. Many books are reviewed, but the editorial board decides not to review others. If a book is not reviewed, it is far from the end of the world. The influence of a book is not determined by whether it is reviewed in any single journal. Scholars generally prefer that their books be reviewed by the journal, but recognize that some may not be.

There is a scholar who wrote a book many, many years ago. For whatever reason, the editorial board at the time decided not to review the book. The author wrote appeal letters not only to the editor, but to practically every official of any stature in the American Psychological Association. When that did not work, he did not give up. He has continued to write over the years, so that every new editor of the journal and new president of APA can be assured of receiving a letter from this individual, complaining about the treatment he received many years ago and demanding that his book be reviewed. This is a man who could not accept even a minor defeat graciously.

❧ Lesson 48 ❧

Realize That the World Is Not Fair

L ET'S CONTINUE with the story of the author whose book was not reviewed. Should his book have been reviewed? I have no idea. It all happened so long ago that the issue has become moot. We are no longer reviewing books published before 2000. But perhaps it should have been. In the course of my career, I have seen countless situations that seemed, to me at least, unfair. Some were only slightly unfair, such as someone winning an award who seemed not to have deserved it, but seemed to have the right connections whereas his or her competitors did not. Others were grossly unfair, such as the case of someone who was turned down for tenure at a major institution and in which someone else whose record was markedly inferior received tenure instead. There were people hired who should not have been, people not hired who should have been, grants funded that should not have been, and grants not funded that should have been. Luck has a way of distributing itself without regard to what people may think they merit.

You will find, over the course of a career, that luck averages out for many people, but not for all people. Chances are you will have some occasions when your luck is better than you expected, other occasions when your luck is worse. But it does not always average out. If you are in a fatal plane crash, as was my friend Joe Rigney, formerly a psychologist with the Navy, then your luck simply ran out for good. If you become ill when you are young, as did the noted paleontologist (and author of *The Mismeasure of Man,* published in 1981) Stephen Gould, you are simply unlucky. Gould was able to

112

fight off cancer early in his life, but then succumbed to it at the relatively early age of 60.

If you believe that life should be fair, you are at substantial risk, I believe, for becoming embittered. The reason is that even if a person's luck averages out, many of us find much more salient the bad luck than the good luck we have. So if we believe life should be fair, we are susceptible to thinking that it is unfair—to us. Don't waste your time. Anyone can find things about which to be bitter or cynical. I certainly can. You are much better off moving on and focusing on the positive things in your life. Research shows that people seem to have relatively stable average levels of happiness. That is, people tend to be happier or less happy people, almost without regard to what happens to them. You will have a more happy life if you follow the oft-given advice that you are about as happy as you make up your mind to be.

One of the more notable examples I have seen is that of a colleague of mine. He and a collaborator invented an important construct in psychology. Someone else then popularized that construct. The individual who popularized the construct has probably received much more credit than the colleague who coinvented the construct. It's just not fair!

If the world of psychology, like the world beyond psychology, is so unfair, why even bother to make an effort to succeed? Well, there are several reasons. First, all systems have unfairness either built into them or as incidental factors. So you can decide to do something else besides academic psychology, but you will soon discover unfairness in the new system you enter too. Second, often things are unfair in the short run, but tend to even out over the long run. So maybe you do not get one thing you want that you should have gotten, but then later, you do get something you wanted that perhaps you should not have gotten. My experience is that over the long run things often (although not always) work out. Third, if

113

everyone gave up when they discovered that the world of psychology can be unfair, there would be no one left in it.

So you need to learn how to survive in systems that are, to a greater or lesser extent, unfair, at least by our perception of them. The sooner you accept the fact that things are not necessarily fair, the sooner you can learn to cope with the way the world is, rather than the way many of us unrealistically wish the world were.

❧ Lesson 49 ❧

Don't Hold Grudges

EARLY IN MY CAREER, I wrote a book that was, at the time, very important to me. It was the book that I hoped would launch my professional career. The publisher sought external reviews before publishing it and, as I recall, two were quite positive. A third one was devastatingly negative. The reviewer wrote 17 single-spaced pages slamming the book and saying, in essence, that the publisher would be crazy to publish it. From what I heard, I was not the first person to be on the receiving end of such treatment from this individual. I was lucky: The publisher chose to disregard the review, suggesting only that I take from the review what I thought would be helpful to me, and published the book. The book later became a "citation classic" of the Institute of Scientific Information.

Although the review was anonymous, it was pretty obvious who wrote it. I was extremely distressed at the time. I was distressed that I was so early in my career, and had already managed to make an enemy. Over the years, I have had many interactions with this individual, including reviewing his papers and books. I had a choice of whether to hold a grudge or to let go of what had happened. I decided to let go. There was no benefit either to me or to the individual in my holding a grudge. Over the years, we have even become friends, although perhaps not close friends. I have gained quite a bit from my interactions with this individual, knowledge that would have been lost to me had I held a grudge. I believed that, whatever the person's flaws, there was a basis for a relationship.

I have been on the receiving end of a grudge, however. Once I noticed that a colleague was acting strangely toward me. This strangeness continued over several years. The colleague seemed almost always to disagree with anything I said, and to criticize me at every opportunity. Our relationship was strained for many years. I finally got up the courage to ask the individual whether something was wrong. This was hard to do, because I was unaware of any interaction that would have caused the colleague to behave in the way he or she did. The colleague at first hemmed and hawed a little, and then the truth came out. Many years ago, the colleague told me, I had written an article that the colleague interpreted as critical of his or her theory. I was flabbergasted. I could not even remember having written such an article.

I had my assistant do a search of my vita, and finally we were able to locate the article that apparently had offended my colleague. I did indeed mention the colleague's theory, but I thought I had done it in a basically favorable light. At the same time, I had expressed a disagreement with aspects of his theory, much as colleagues have expressed disagreement with mine. I spoke again to the colleague and explained that I certainly had not intended to derogate the colleague or the colleague's work. Eventually, we patched things up and even have become somewhat close. Holding a grudge is good for no one!

I work with a colleague from another institution in one of my official roles who seems to have no limit to the number of grudges he holds. He lashes out at people for the smallest reason, and seems to delight in petty revenge. He is a bitter malcontent, disliked by all the colleagues with whom he works. This is not a fate to aspire to. If you are one to hold grudges, you will find plenty of reasons to bear grudges, and plenty of people against whom to bear them. Heck, many, if not most of my colleagues who have reviewed my work at one time or another have not liked something I have written. Indeed, sometimes I have later not liked things I have written. The best advice: Get through whatever issues you have with someone, then move on. There is so much to life. Don't waste it being bitter.

❧ Lesson 50 ❧

Stay Away From
Exploiters and Parasites

IN ANY FIELD, there are people who will want to exploit you and there are people who, quite simply, are parasites. Exploiters look at relations with you totally in terms of what they can get out of the relationship. Usually, they are in positions of greater power than you are. Parasites include exploiters, but also people who are in positions of equal or lesser power. What exploiters and all parasites have in common is their viewing relationships as wholly instrumental and one-directional—that is, in terms of what they can get out of you.

I have made a conscious decision to stay away from such people. The issue with them is not one of misunderstanding or of a lesson that both can learn: These people, in my experience, are dispositionally parasitic. And they do not change. There is an old maxim: "Fool me once, shame on you; fool me twice, shame on me." This maxim applies in relationships with such people. Continuing to interact with them, unless you absolutely have to, means there is not only a problem with them, but also, a problem with you.

Sometimes, it is difficult to be rid of such people. For example, occasionally, such a person will be an academic advisor. In most programs, it is possible to change advisors. Other times, the person may be a department chair. Such a situation is extremely difficult and one can only hope that the individual will not last in the position. Or one can think of moving. Usually, one can and should make the decision to stay away.

I'm not beyond falling into this trap. I once had a relationship with someone who was a parasite, but because I liked the person, I did not let go. Eventually, I realized I had no choice. The relationship was destructive to me, and had no real value. I let go.

❧ Lesson 51 ❧

Luck Seems To Come in Streaks— Both Bad and Good

GILOVICH, VALLONE, AND TVERSKY (1985) studied what is sometimes called the "hot-hand" phenomenon—the tendency for athletes, such as basketball players, to have runs of good luck. They found out that the runs are in the eyes of the beholders: They are not real. In your career, you may find— as I have—that luck does seem to run in streaks. We have gone through periods in which almost every grant proposal we wrote got funded, and we felt that we had finally hit our stride. Then we have gone through periods in which nothing we wrote got funded—in which it seemed like just putting our names on proposals was enough to doom them. During the dry spells, giving up often seems like the only option.

Sometimes the bad luck is personal. You may have one illness followed by another illness followed by another, or you may lose one important person in your life after another. It seems as though you have been personally selected for bad luck.

Don't give up. Instead, take a look at a table of random numbers. Chances are that you will see many more runs of the same digit than you ever would expect. Why is it that people even need tables of random numbers, or computer generated strings of random numbers? The reason is that people are absolutely terrible at generating them. They put into their strings far fewer runs than would exist in a string of truly random numbers. So there will be periods when things seem to be up or down very often. It never lasts forever, anymore than the stock market ever stays permanently high—or low.

❊ Lesson 52 ❊

Realize That Even if the Tower
Is "Ivory," It Is Not "White"

WHEN I ENTERED ACADEMIA, I expected a life that never quite happened. I thought academics were primarily interested in ideas, put their personal feelings aside in debates, were generous in praise and kind in criticism, and on and on. No such luck. Most of the people I've dealt with are decent people. But some of them aren't. Some are arrogant. Some are selfish. Some are deceitful. And some even are destructive of others, for no obvious reason.

Dealing with such people is never easy. The best advice, really, is to avoid them if you can. That's always my first option. Sometimes the people are not so easily avoidable. If the person is your advisor, consider switching advisors. If the person is your department chair, consider whether there is any member of the university administration whom you can trust and speak to in confidence. But at the same time, realize that this strategy carries risks: The person you thought you could trust might, in fact, prove not to be trustworthy. If the person is a research collaborator, try to get through the current project and then never collaborate with him or her again.

It is not just people who can be disappointing. So can institutions. I have seen many people who are long loyal to their institutions, and then discover that the loyalty goes one way. One retired professor who spent almost his entire career at a state university is suing the university, which seems determined to rob him of the retirement he deserves. Another person got into trouble with his university when an unjustified complaint was filed against him, and the university seemingly sided with the complainant. I have learned it pays to keep one's expectations for loyalty on the part of one's institution relatively modest.

Part of the problem is that it is not exactly the university that acts, but the people behind it. The same is true of any organization. I once had an extremely rewarding relationship with a company for which I did consulting. I found myself becoming very loyal to the organization. The organization was bought by another one, and the new management dropped me like a hot potato. The organization kept its old name but the personnel were completely different. Institutions often get through bad management, but your relationship with the institution may or may not. Institutions are rarely better than the people in them, and when the people change, an institution that may at one time have been great can do downhill pretty fast. At the same time, institutions also can go uphill pretty fast.

One of the most painful experiences one has in academia—and in life in general—is betrayal. People whom one considered close colleagues may betray one, as when something one said in confidence is then disseminated as though one had asked not that it be held in confidence, but rather, be trumpeted on the front page of the local newspaper. If you betray people, you will soon enough find yourself with no one to betray, because no one will trust you. If someone betrays you in a professional relationship, my advice is that you not wait for it to happen a second time. If you continue to trust that person, you are setting yourself up for further disasters.

I am surprised by the extent to which people sometimes dig their own graves (and I must admit that I have sometimes done it myself). Remember, "Fool me once, shame on you; fool me twice, shame on me." Some people let themselves be fooled once, twice, thrice, and onward. They let one or more other people take advantage of them, and then do it again and again. Don't be one of those people. If someone mistreats you, do what you can to avoid being sucked into the same situation again.

❦ Lesson 53 ❦

Help Each Person Find His or Her Own Niche

I LEARNED THIS LESSON from Gordon Bower, my graduate advisor. Gordon has had many graduate students who distinguished themselves in their careers, perhaps more than anyone else that one can readily think of. One of the reasons is that he allowed each graduate student to find his or her own niche. Although he was happy to have students work on his own line of investigation, he was equally happy to let them find their own distinct pursuit.

Students do their best and most creative work when they really love what they do. For this reason, I have encouraged my students to find something they really love. It may be related to something I already am doing, but then, it may not be. What works best for them, in the long run, works best for me.

It is important to realize that niche-finding applies to jobs as well as research. Some years ago, one of my graduate students received two job offers, one from a very highly prestigious academic institution and the other from a less prestigious one. The second one was well-known, but the first one was near the top of the academic pecking order. She asked me which job offer I thought she should take.

The answer might seem straightforward: Why not take the more prestigious offer? But it was not straightforward. The reason is that the kinds of interests she had seemed better to fit the somewhat less prestigious place. In particular, she liked teaching quite a bit, and the second place seemed to emphasize teaching more than the first one.

I was young and foolish at the time—barely out of my 20s—and I gave her bad advice. I told her to take the more prestigious offer. She did, and it proved to be a mistake. She did not fit in. Several years later, she left, and eventually she ended up at a place that particularly values teaching.

The lesson learned, of course, is that students and everyone else need to find a place where they fit. Fit is much more important than prestige. If one finds the right fit, one will do one's best work, and things will generally go as they should from there. In seeking a job, it is much more important to find out about what the institution values than it is to find out about what their rank order is in some set of ratings. If you and they value the same things, you are likely to be happy. If you and they don't have the same values, you are unlikely to be happy, regardless of the institution's prestige.

As a mentor, friend, or colleague, do not use fear as your primary way of motivating people. Some people do what they do not because it is what they care about, but because they are afraid of what will happen if they don't do it. They may be trying to fulfill their parents' wishes, or their significant other's, or their department chair's, or their mentor's or whoever's. People rarely find their true niche when motivated primarily by fear. Nor do they do their best work. Whenever possible, encourage people to do something because they believe in it, not because they are afraid of what will happen to them if they don't.

❧ Lesson 54 ❧

Remember That Institutional Cultures Are Slow To Change

SINCE I FIRST ARRIVED at Yale as an undergraduate in 1968, many things have changed. The people are mostly different, the physical plant has improved, the course offerings have changed, some departments that once existed no longer exist and other departments have been created. So much has changed!

But what has not changed—and what often is slowest to change—is the institutional culture. Yale still values teaching of undergraduates highly. It still does things for the community less frequently than it probably should. It still has wonderful cultural attractions.

It is not just Yale, of course. I have been to various institutions over the years, sometimes repeatedly, and have been struck by how the most basic aspects of organizational cultures are very slow to change (Sternberg, 2000). If you are thinking of going to a place, and they tell you that it is in a period of transition, watch out. A place that values mediocrity will not change so fast, if only because the people there will continue to hire mediocre people who do not compete with them. A place that values excellence (and I think Yale is one of them) probably will continue to value excellence, because it will look for the best people it can find. A place that is institutionally bureaucratic will probably stay that way, because it often would take the bureaucracy to reform itself, and most bureaucracies are slow to do so. Thus, if you are promised change, be at least a little wary of what is likely to change and what is not.

❧ Lesson 55 ❧

Give What You Hope To Get

THE LESSON "give what you hope to get" may sound like the Golden Rule. It is. I have found that, on average, you pretty much get in proportion to what you give in a career, and that what goes around comes around. If you are nice to other people, in the long run, most of them probably will be nice to you. If you are nasty, in the long run, they probably won't be very nice to you either.

A problem with academia is that, superficially, at least, it sometimes seems more to value getting than giving. Just as successful business people may hoard money, successful academics may hoard honors to place on their vitas, cushy trips abroad, light teaching loads, or whatever. Human nature is probably no different as a function of the occupation people are in. But if you look at the most successful people in academia, among whom I count my own mentors, they are people who have given a great deal. Indeed, I doubt that, among the most successful people, one would find many who were selfish in their professional lives. They learned, one way or another, that you get back what you give.

I once was asked to meet with a team of visitors to Yale. I was busy at the time and felt like the last thing I needed was yet another meeting. But it was important to the university and the group for me to have the meeting. I had it, expecting nothing in return. What I got in return was the establishment of a collaboration that has proved to be one of the best I've ever had. You give even a little, and you may be surprised by how much you get in return.

125

❧ Lesson 56 ❧

Understand the Benefits and Limits of Loyalty

O NE OF THE THINGS in which we most take pride at the PACE Center is loyalty. Even before this center started, one of the things I valued most in my graduate students and postdocs was loyalty. I have always rewarded it, and still do. I think many other professionals in the field feel the same way.

What do I mean by loyalty? It has a rather complex meaning, at least in an academic context. If a person is loyal, it means that I can trust that person implicitly. I can be confident that they say what they believe and that they mean what they say. The person is also trustworthy in action. I know that when they represent us to others, they will do so in a fair and, I hope, in a reasonably positive light. They will work for us in the same way that we will work for them. They expect our relationship with them to be symmetrical: They expect to get in proportion to what they give. And they will never stab us in the back.

At the same time, I do not expect students or employees to lose opportunities to profit from others. Most of my primary advisees also work with other faculty members—and should. By working with several faculty members, they receive a variety of perspectives, rather than just one. And they can bring those diverse perspectives to bear on our work at the PACE Center as well as elsewhere.

Some people are reluctant to criticize friends or colleagues because they are afraid it will be perceived as disloyal. The opposite is true. If you are loyal to someone, you will tell them their strengths as well as their weaknesses, and give them the honest feedback loyalty merits.

Sometimes, unfortunately, the loyalty you bestow upon another is not reciprocated. You act toward the other in what you believe to be an honest and loyal way, and you are poorly repaid for it. In such cases, the answer is not to be disloyal toward the person as that person was toward you, but rather, to eliminate or at least minimize to the extent possible your relationship with that person. People who are double-crossers rarely do it just once. If someone is willing to admit to an error and pledges to do better next time, sure, give the person another chance. But if it happens again, you can expect it will keep happening, again and again.

I have a colleague who once was stabbed in the back by someone with whom he had worked very closely. The backstab came as a total surprise. My colleague had been very loyal to the individual, and then, the individual spread a nasty lie about my colleague. What's sad is that the colleague had been warned by others of the man's treacherous nature, but had not wanted to listen. Listen! Often, others see things that you just do not want to see.

❧ Lesson 57 ❧

Pick Important Problems on Which To Work

LIKE MANY OTHER PSYCHOLOGISTS, I have spent long days attending conventions and other meetings where I would sit in on presentations and symposia whose only conceivable interest seemed to be that the presentation of the paper by the author may have paved the way for him or her to get funding to attend the conference. But, of course, excruciatingly boring material is not limited to conferences (or, occasionally, books of advice!). If you open the pages of a typical journal, you may find the typical issue contains only a few articles of interest to you, with at least some of the other articles defying any guess as to who would have wanted to spend the time to study whatever the authors thought they were studying.

Why do some people devote so many resources to problems of so little interest to anyone but themselves and perhaps a handful of others? And how can they be satisfied writing articles that few people will read and giving talks that few people will want to listen to? One possibility is that there is a problem in our system of graduate education. I think that a major problem in this system is that we place so much emphasis on how to solve problems that, at times, we forget about the importance of selecting good problems in the first place. The result is that the work that is done is often very fine and careful work on problems of little interest.

There is another possibility why an individual might pursue a problem that is interesting to him or her but to few others. That individual may see merit in a problem that others simply do not yet see. We need always to remember that our judgments are, at bottom, nothing more than judgments. Some of the best work in the field has been that which opens up new problem areas that earlier had been neglected. So there is always the possibility that a problem that seems uninteresting at one point will seem interesting at another. For example, the problem of the nature of consciousness has gone in and out of fashion in psychology, at times seeming central, at other times seeming peripheral, and at still other times (as in the heyday of behaviorism) not seeming to be a real problem at all.

How can you tell if a problem is interesting, scientifically or otherwise? There is no guaranteed way of knowing, but there are certainly steps you can take to gauge interest. A first thing you can do is to try to state—preferably in writing— why anyone in his or her right mind should be interested in the problem. If you cannot think of reasons, that may be a bad sign. Most speakers and many article-writers seem to leave it to their audience to figure out why the problem is important. Don't! Figure it out and state it for yourself. A second thing you can do is to try briefly describing the problem and why you think it is important to psychologists who do *not* specialize in your field. Ask them frankly if they think the problem is interesting, and why or why not? A third thing you can do is to explain it to a layperson who has no training whatsoever in psychology. Does this individual find the work interesting?

Some psychologists would say that it does not matter what laypeople think. I think it matters. First, laypeople often have the best sense of what problems are boring, because they have no vested interest in what psychologists do. Second, laypeople are the ones who decide what money is to be allocated for research funding (e.g., Congress people). Third, when you teach psychology to undergraduate students, you are teaching to laypeople. If the research they learn about is boring, why will they want to pursue psychology as a field beyond the first course they take in it?

129

Zuckerman (1983) found that the most distinguished scientists were distinguished by virtue of their taste in problems. I thus emphasize with my own students that the most important issue they can confront is not how to solve a problem, but whether the problem is even worth solving in the first place. It is important to solve problems well. But if the problems are not worth solving, it matters little how you solve them!

Sometimes in choosing problems, there is a tendency among some laypersons, and even some psychologists, to believe that the more complex something is, the more impressive it is. I have found in my career, however, that often the simplest ideas are the ones that have the most power.

For example, two of the greatest psychologists of the generation of psychologists before me would certainly be Amos Tversky and Daniel Kahneman. They achieved their greatest fame, perhaps, for their work on heuristics and biases. For example, they showed how often people will use what they called the availability heuristic (Tversky & Kahneman, 1973), which is simply the recalling to mind of information one has heard recently or often. The idea is simple, the experiments they used to demonstrate the heuristic were simple, and yet the idea proved to have extraordinary power in explaining, at some level, many puzzling phenomena in the judgment and decision-making literature as well as many puzzles in everyday life, such as why people are more afraid of plane than of car crashes, even though many more people die in car than in plane crashes. According to Tversky and Kahneman, their greater fear is due to information about plane crashes being much more prominent in the media, and therefore being more easily retrievable, than information about car crashes.

The point is that often the simplest ideas are the most powerful. I have often felt that if I cannot explain what I am working on in a couple of sentences, then something is wrong.

130

Of course, I could also explain it in a book. But the core idea should be easily explicable. That is the elegance of Tversky and Kahneman's work. So when choosing a problem, go for the important problem. You may find that it is important not because it is so complex, but rather, because it is so simple.

❦ Lesson 58 ❦

Create Your Own Style of Work To Distinguish Yourself From the Rest

WHEN YOU START OUT in a career, you are often happy to have even one idea to pursue. As you proceed through your career, chances are you will have a variety of problems available for you to tackle, and you may need to decide which one or ones are worthy of your attention. I believe that a major factor in deciding what to do is to find something that can distinguish you from the pack.

The best psychologists have a distinctive style. It cannot be hidden. Often, their work can be reviewed via "masked review," in which their identity is not revealed; but it is nevertheless obvious who did the work. Why? Because they have a particular way of thinking about problems, doing research, or writing up their research that sets them apart from others.

Most academics in the sciences know how to design studies, analyze data, write up studies. If you want to make a distinctive contribution to the field, you need to figure out something that sets you apart from everyone else. Often, this means coming up with your own distinctive way of doing things. There is not a one-size-fits-all way of doing things. Sometimes journal editors seem to go out of their way to homogenize the products of research, but fortunately, they do not entirely succeed. We each find our own way.

For example, my own style tends to involve coming up with some fairly large-scale theory (e.g., the theory of successful intelligence or the triangular theory of love), and then finding diverse ways of testing that theory. The research I do thus uses converging empirical operations. I tend to collabo-

132

rate a lot with graduate students and postdoctoral students, but less with undergraduate students. Those are aspects of a style that works for me. Styles of work are not right or wrong. You may prefer larger theories or smaller theories; or someone else's theories; or you may prefer a biological approach of one kind or another. You may prefer working with undergraduates rather than graduate students, or you may not have graduate students available to work with. What is important is to use experience to find ways of working with which you are comfortable, and which permit you to express yourself through your work.

I believe that the work an academic psychologist does can be as much an art as a science. The science, of course, is in the research. But the art is in finding a means of creative expression that sets you apart, much as an artist develops a unique style that sets him or herself apart from other artists who might paint the same subjects. Two artists can paint the same subject but produce paintings that look very different, even though each painting reflects the same external reality. Scientists are no different. They bring their own artistic mode of expression to their science.

⚛ Lesson 59 ⚛

Be Guided by Problems, Not Methods or Fields

IT IS SAID that carpenters will always find things on which to use a hammer. The metaphor suggests that we all have sets of tools and then look for problems that can be solved using these tools. The downside of this approach is that we tend to ignore or shun anything that does not lend itself to, well, hammering, or whatever kind of work we do. So we may pass up countless opportunities, just because our hammer does not lend itself to these opportunities. People become fixated on methods, or on fields, rather than on problems.

Field fixation can be as damaging to the understanding of psychological phenomena as is methodological fixation (Sternberg & Grigorenko, 2001). Psychology is divided into areas such as biological psychology, clinical psychology, cognitive psychology, developmental psychology, industrial–organizational psychology, social psychology, personality psychology, and so forth. Departments often organize the specializations of their professors in this way; graduate programs are usually structured in this way; and jobs are typically advertised in this way. This organization of the field, departments, graduate programs, and jobs is less than optimal. It encourages division rather than unification.

Several factors play a role in maintaining the current suboptimal organization of psychology:

Tradition. First, and foremost, it is the way things have been done for a long time. When a system of organization is entrenched, people tend to accept it as a given. For example, most psychology departments have chairpersons, but members of those departments probably do not spend a lot of time questioning whether they should have chairpersons—they just accept this system of organization. Of course, new fields within psychology come and go. For example, the fields of evolutionary psychology and health psychology are relative newcomers to the roster of fields of psychology. They will either become part of the standard organization of the field, or slowly disappear.

Vested interest. Second, once a discipline such as psychology has been organized in a certain way, people in the discipline acquire a vested interest in maintaining that organization, much as people gain a vested interest in maintaining any system that seemingly has worked for them in the past. For example, most cognitive psychologists were trained as cognitive psychologists, or personality psychologists as personality psychologists. Were the field suddenly to reorganize, current scholars and practitioners might quickly find themselves without the kind of knowledge base and even socially organized field of inquiry that would allow them to continue to function successfully.

The need to specialize. Third, no one can specialize in everything. Students of psychology need to specialize in some way, and structuring psychology in terms of fields has been viewed as a sensible way to define specializations. Thus, someone who specializes in social psychology will be expected to know about a series of related phenomena such as impression formation, attribution, and stereotyping. Or someone who specializes in cognitive psychology will be expected to know about a set of related phenomena such as perception, memory, and thinking. And successively greater levels of specialization ultimately may be encouraged, such as in cognitive approaches to memory, to implicit memory, or to the use of priming methodology in studying implicit memory.

I believe that the current organization of the field is distinctly suboptimal and even maladaptive. There are several reasons for this belief (Sternberg & Grigorenko, 2001).

The field could be organized better to understand psychological phenomena. Examples of psychological phenomena include memory, intelligence, dyslexia, attachment, creativity, prejudice, and amnesia, among others. None of these phenomena are best studied within a specialized field of psychology.

For example, although memory can be investigated as a cognitive phenomenon, it can, and should be, studied through the techniques of several other fields. These fields include biological psychology and cognitive neuroscience (e.g., in attempts to find out where in the brain memories are stored), clinical psychology (e.g., in the conflict over repressed memories), social psychology (e.g., in preferential memory for self-referential memories), behavioral genetics (e.g., in the heritability of memory characteristics), to name just some of the relevant fields. Someone studying memory only through one approach or set of techniques will understand only part of the phenomenon.

Similarly, extraversion can be, and has been, studied from personality, differential, biological, cognitive, social, cultural, and other points of view. Someone studying extraversion from only one of these points of view—let's say, personality—almost certainly will understand the phenomenon only in a narrow way, in terms of, say, extraversion as a trait, without fully appreciating the role of biological or cognitive processes, or of culture, for that matter.

The same argument can be applied to virtually any psychological phenomenon. By subsuming psychological phenomena under fields of psychology, the discipline encourages a narrow view rather than a broad approach to understanding psychological phenomena. But you will do better work if you take a broad approach to phenomena, and educate yourself broadly so that you are able to take such an approach.

Organizing by fields can isolate individuals who study the same phenomena. Two individuals within a psychology department may both study attachment, for example, but if one is in personality psychology and another in developmental psychology, they may have little interaction. This is because in a typical department, students and professors are located next to—and attend the same meetings and read the same journals as—others in their field regardless of the phenomena being studied.

The current organization may create false oppositions between individuals or groups studying phenomena from different vantage points. Here's an example: Individuals studying memory from a cognitive perspective may never quite understand the work of those studying memory from a clinical standpoint; this can lead to a sense of hostility toward the viewpoints of those who do not understand their "preferred" way of studying memory. Or individuals studying love from social-psychological versus clinical points of view may (and sometimes do) see themselves in opposition, as though there were a uniquely correct approach to studying a psychological phenomenon.

The current system tends to marginalize psychological phenomena that fall outside the boundaries of a specific field. For example, psychological phenomena such as imagination, motivation, or emotion may tend to be ignored in a department if they are not seen as part of the "core" of a field. This also extends to the people studying such phenomena. They may have difficulty getting hired because hiring is often done by area, and the people studying phenomena at the interface of fields of psychology may be perceived as not fitting neatly into any one area. In turn, faculty in a given area may not want to hire such people if they feel that they will not get the full benefit of a slot or that such individuals will not contribute adequately to graduate (or even undergraduate) training in that so-called "core" field.

Research may tilt toward issues to which a limited set of tools may be applied. The current system essentially equips students with a set of tools (e.g., the methods of developmental psychology, or cognitive neuroscience, or social psychology, or mathematical psychology). Instead of being driven by substantive issues, the system then encourages students to go in search of a phenomenon for which they can use their tools, much in the way a carpenter might seek to find objects for which he or she can use a hammer.

The current system can discourage new ways of studying problems. If someone wishes to educate students in terms of the existing boundaries of fields, they will encounter little problem. But if they want to cross those boundaries, other faculty may worry that the individual will not be properly trained in a field, or may have trouble getting a job, or may not fit into the departmental structure. And in truth, they may be justified in all these concerns.

Finally, and perhaps most importantly, the traditional disciplinary approach of largely subsuming psychological phenomena under fields of study, rather than the other way around, leads psychologists to confuse aspects of phenomena with the phenomena as a whole. This confusion is analogous to the use of synecdoche in speech, in which one substitutes a part for a whole (e.g., "crown" for "kingdom"), except that unlike poets or other writers, psychologists are unaware of their use of this device. The psychologists believe they are studying the whole phenomenon when in fact they are studying only a small part of it.

Consider the well-worn parable of the blind men each touching a different part of the elephant and each being convinced that he is touching a different animal. In psychology, the situation is like always touching the same part of a phenomenon and thinking that this part tells you all you need to know to understand the whole phenomenon. Here are two examples:

In the study of human intelligence, psychometricians may keep discovering a "general factor" and thus become convinced that the general factor largely "explains" intelligence. Biological psychologists may find a spot or two in the brain that lights up during the fMRI or PET-scan analysis of the commission of cognitive tasks and become convinced that these parts of the brain fully explain intelligence. Cultural psychologists may find wide cultural differences in notions of the nature of intelligence, and become convinced that intelligence is best explained simply as a cultural invention. Each psychologist touches a different part of the metaphorical elephant, and becomes convinced that part represents the whole (and fairly simple) animal.

In general, scientists who are not well trained in one another's techniques are likely to be suspicious of the other's techniques and of the conclusions drawn from them. Instead, these scientists probably will continue to do research within their own paradigm, which keeps supporting their views and thereby reinforces their confidence that they are right and that those who adhere to a paradigm from some other field are misguided.

A more sensible and psychologically justifiable way of organizing psychology as a discipline, and in departments and graduate study in psychology, is in terms of psychological phenomena. We have advocated this different way of organizing the discipline of psychology because psychological phenomena are not arbitrary, but the so-called fields of psychology largely are (Sternberg & Grigorenko, 2001).

Under this approach, an individual might choose to specialize in a set of related phenomena, such as learning and memory, or stereotyping and prejudice, or motivation and emotion, and then study the phenomenon or phenomena of interest from multiple points of view. The individual thus would reach a fuller understanding of the phenomenon being studied because he or she would not be limited by a set of assumptions or methods drawn from only one field of psychology.

Our proposal carries with it several advantages that are largely complementary to the disadvantages of the present field-based approach that currently dominates the discipline. People might very well end up specializing in several related psychological phenomena, but they would understand these phenomena broadly rather than narrowly, which is certainly an advantage if one's goal is comprehensive psychological understanding. Psychology would be less susceptible to tendencies that field-based organization encourages: narrowness, isolation, false oppositions, marginalization, largely method-driven rather than phenomenon-driven approaches to research, discouragement of new ways of approaching psychological phenomena, and confusion of the part with the whole.

❧ Lesson 60 ❧

Be Patient About Making a Difference

A MAJOR GOAL I have set for myself is to change the way education is done in the United States. In particular, I believe that the way we educate children in the United States tends to benefit children who are strong in memory and analytical abilities, but to place at a disadvantage children whose strengths are in creative and practical abilities.

How far have I gotten toward achieving my goals? Not very far, really. At times, I have been terribly frustrated. Here I am 55 years of age, and I have had very little impact on changing education in the United States. There are days when I wonder why I bother even to try. Then I remember the advice of my undergraduate mentor, Endel Tulving, who once said to me that people tend vastly to underestimate the amount of time it takes to get any meaningful kind of change to take place. His words have kept me going at times when I have felt that my efforts to change education—or anything else, really—have stalled or even hit a dead end.

When we are young, we often believe that we can change things pretty quickly, if only we set our minds to it. Then we encounter resistance from many quarters, and may become discouraged that tasks that we thought would be easy are much harder than we ever expected. Often the opposition we encounter seems misguided. For some reason, people don't acknowledge the sublime rationality and reasonableness of what we suggest. But remember Tulving's advice. It can take a substantial amount of time even to get fairly simple and straightforward things to change in a positive way. And remember as well that the courses of action that appear reasonable to you may appear to be anything but reasonable to someone else.

❦ Lesson 61 ❦

When You Can't Start but Have To, Start Small

ONE OF THE UNHAPPIER but also more common experiences in academic research is getting stuck. It may be in starting to write or revise a paper or a book, in preparing a lecture, or in anything else.

Some years ago I signed a contract to write an introductory psychology textbook. I set a deadline for starting on the text. It came and went, and nothing happened. So I set myself another deadline. That deadline also passed without even a word's making its way onto paper. I then set a third deadline and decided that this time I meant it. But as the deadline approached, the task seemed so daunting that I felt paralyzed and could not see my way through to starting the writing of the book.

I then realized that I had to redefine the problem. I had planned to start the book from the beginning, beginning with chapter 1, which was to be on the nature of psychology. But the first chapter of an introductory psychology text is often one of the most difficult to write. I was setting myself up for failure. Then I decided to change strategy. I asked myself which chapter would be absolutely the easiest one to write, and I settled on the chapter on intelligence, because that is my main area of expertise. So I started writing the chapter on intelligence, and that was a task I could handle. Then, after that chapter was done, I took on the second easiest chapter, that on thinking, another area about which I felt well-informed. Again, I was able to complete the chapter without too much difficulty. By now I was well underway and no longer had to do the chapters in order of ease. But by starting with the easiest task, I made it possible for me to get started and then to have the motivation to keep going.

✣ Lesson 62 ✣

Don't Procrastinate

FOR SOME REASON, many academics are serious procrastina-
tors. They save things until the last minute, and, even then,
often procrastinate further. My beginning the introductory psychology text was one example. But a more telling example
was revising a paper I had submitted to a journal.

I wrote a paper on a certain form of reasoning called
linear-syllogistic reasoning. Linear-syllogism problems are
ones such as "John is taller than Mary. Mary is taller than
Susan. Who is tallest?" I submitted the paper and, after a very
long waiting period, got it back with requests for numerous
major revisions.

I was very discouraged by the reviews. Although the
paper was not rejected outright, the amount of work that
would be needed to revise the paper seemed to me to be
inordinate. It might take me days or even a week to revise
the darn thing. So I put the paper aside, waiting for a large
block of time to work on it. As time went by, it became clear
that the large block of time was never to come. There always
seemed to be something else to do, and there were so many
interruptions and disruptions of my work schedule that it
became clear that the paper might be in permanent cold
storage.

One day, I decided that I would just do as much of the
revision as I could. To my astonishment, I finished the revision
in a day. Now, I can't say many things take less time than I
expect. That is not the lesson. The lesson is that by endlessly
procrastinating, I had delayed publication of a major article,
and for no reason. I now try not to procrastinate. All procrasti-
nation does is increase anxiety and the feeling that one cannot

144

do whatever one is delaying. It is much better, when one has a forbidding task facing one, just to get the task done.

When I edit a book, I ask a variety of scholars to contribute to it. In any project, there is almost always some author who waits until the last minute or beyond, thinking that he or she will be able to get it done at the last minute. These people just are never on time for anything. I have discovered that one can wait up to a point, but after that, one is better off moving ahead with publication of the book, without the chapters of such authors. I then do not ask these individuals to contribute again. Once you get a reputation as a procrastinator, you may find that few people take you seriously.

Scientific products, like refrigerated products in a supermarket, have a "shelf life." A study that is of interest at a given time may, one year later, be dated or even "expired." You need to get data out while they are "hot." So when you do scientific work, do not procrastinate in getting it "to market." If you procrastinate too long, by the time you get the work out, it may be too late.

Many years ago, I had a student who was often a good worker, but he was the kind of person who would never do today what he could put off until tomorrow. He did a study that was quite nice, and that would address an issue that, at the time, was quite hot in the literature. I told him that the issue on which he was working was hot, but that it would not stay at the forefront forever. He finally did get around to submitting his work, but by the time he did, the field had already progressed, and his work no longer had the impact it would have had if he had submitted it in a timely fashion.

❧ Lesson 63 ❧

Maintain Your Good Reputation

I N ACADEMIA, the most valuable thing you possess is not some computer or piece of lab equipment, but rather, your reputation. Careers are made or broken on the basis of reputations. You therefore should do all you can to protect your reputation. One thing you can do is to fulfill the commitments you make. If you become perceived as someone who "punks out," you will find fewer and fewer people asking you to do anything.

I remember being on a selection committee for an international conference, and the name of a distinguished scholar came up. Everyone would have liked to invite the scholar, and as it was a prestigious conference, perhaps the scholar also would have liked to be invited. We decided not to invite her, however, not because we did not think she would be a good speaker, but because she had acquired a reputation for making and then not fulfilling commitments. And when she broke commitments, it usually was at the last minute, after it was too late to get someone else in her place. She had hurt her own reputation through not fulfilling commitments. Don't do the same with your reputation.

Nonfulfillment can take the form of breaking commitments, or of meeting them in a mediocre way. If you agree to do something, give it your best. Otherwise, don't bother. You will acquire a good reputation if you give the jobs you undertake your best effort.

There are many ways to harm your reputation—harassing people, exploiting people, and acting in other unprofessional ways. Once you give up your reputation, you give up your most important asset in the field.

❧ Lesson 64 ❧

What May Seem Like
a Crushing Blow Now May Later
Seem Like a Little Tap

I N THE COURSE of a normal career, you will encounter many successes, but also many failures. At the time, some of these failures may seem spectacular. I mentioned earlier the time I thought I had a job offer from another university, told Yale I did, and then found I didn't. All I wanted to do was duck my head in the sand. At another point in my career, I seemed to be building up a stream of rejections of articles that would set a world record. When such things happen, they may seem like the end of the world. You may feel like quitting. Don't! What seems like a world-shattering failure at one point, in retrospect, years, months, or sometimes, even weeks later, will not seem so important. You just have to get through these difficult times with all the dignity you can preserve.

Often, you will feel like other people are thinking about and talking about nothing other than your failures. Chances are that you are exaggerating other people's interest in you. But the passage of time cures many wounds. Just let time take its course, and above all, preserve your dignity in doing so.

Many of the most successful writers, artists, and scientists have had stunningly bad periods in their lives. They have endured deaths in the family, major public scandals, failures of their work to be appreciated, and on the list goes. But the ones who "made it" did not give up. I noticed at one point that many novels by one of my favorite writers, Dean Koontz,

147

were reissues of novels that had been published earlier under a different title. At first, I was puzzled. Then I figured out what had happened. The novels were published before Koontz became a best-selling writer. In those days, they did not sell much. Now, when they were reissued under new titles, they were having great success. Imagine the loss to the world if Koontz had given up in the face of low sales.

❦ Lesson 65 ❦

Most Things Take Longer
Than You Think They Will

IT IS COMMON in a career to discover that things take longer, and often quite a bit longer, than you expect they will. For this reason, it is important to begin projects, especially those with a short deadline, in a timely fashion. Otherwise, you risk missing deadlines. Endel Tulving once told me this, and he proved to be dead-on accurate.

I think I first discovered this lesson in its full force in my first year of teaching. I was teaching four semester courses that year—two each semester—plus attempting to do administrative chores for the department and also do new research and write up my dissertation as a book. I further had this idea that I could teach a course on intelligence, and use the lectures to write a book on theories of intelligence.

So each day, I set aside some time to prepare the lectures in a format that later could serve as a book. But as the semester wore on, I got further and further behind on the book. I could barely keep up with the lectures. Eventually, I realized that I just could not keep up with the lectures in a format that would make them a book. That was in 1975. I did eventually write the book. It was published 15 years later, in 1990! I no longer try simultaneously to teach a course and create books from the lectures I give. Things take longer than one thinks.

❧ Lesson 66 ❧

Remember That
Acceptance Is Not Necessarily Good,
Rejection Not Necessarily Bad

AFTER I HAD GOTTEN my paper on linear-syllogistic reasoning (mentioned earlier) accepted, I did a study on the development of linear-syllogistic reasoning. I was looking at what changed in children's information processing with age. I did a study on the subject and submitted it to a journal.

After submitting the article, I found myself regretting that I had sent it to the journal. The more I thought about the study, the more trivial it seemed. All I had done was to take a paradigm I had used among adults, and apply it with minor modifications to children of different ages. There seemed to be little original in such a study, and I began to worry that I would embarrass myself with the submission. I considered withdrawing the submission, and then decided that instead I would let the study get rejected and die a natural death.

A few months later I got the reviews back on the article, and to my astonishment, I received three very positive reviews and was required to make only the most minor revisions to get the article published.

In contrast, I once submitted an article on an aspect of thinking to a second-string journal, figuring that it would not have a chance with a better journal. The article was rejected with rather scathing reviews that I felt were unfair. I decided to submit the article to a better journal, and to my surprise, the better journal accepted the article with few revisions.

One would like to believe that good articles and grant proposals get accepted and bad ones get rejected. But although, on average, better articles or proposals are more likely to get accepted than bad ones, there are many factors that affect the ultimate fate of an article or proposal. I learned long ago to take editorial actions more or less with a grain of salt. The articles and proposals that are easiest to get accepted are often ones like my article on the development of linear-syllogistic reasoning: The article makes a modest contribution and, most importantly, offends no one. Often more important pieces of work do offend someone, so they are more likely to be rejected. Indeed, I believe that the work that is most likely to be rejected is that which is very bad, in which case it is rejected because it is very bad, and that which is very good, in which case it is rejected because it threatens someone. Ultimately, you need to become your best judge and do what you do not because it pleases someone else, but because it pleases you.

When I was a graduate student, Endel Tulving and I wrote an article on the measurement of subjective organization in free recall. We worked hard on the article and thought it was a pretty good article. We submitted the article to the *Psychological Bulletin*. To my great consternation, the article was rejected. It was only my second major submission to a journal, and I already felt like a failure.

Later, I was writing another article on subjective organization, and I asked Tulving how I should cite the article that we had had rejected. He told me to cite it as "Rejected by *Psychological Bulletin*." I couldn't believe what I was hearing. Here we had the embarrassment and ignominy of having an article rejected, and he wanted me to advertise it to the world!

At the time, I did not understand. Now I do. He thought it was a good paper, and I thought it was a good paper, and that was good enough for him. He was convinced that the paper was good, regardless of what the reviewers said, and he was willing to flaunt it. His pride was in his work, not in the journal that accepted or did not accept it.

P.S. It later was accepted by *Psychological Bulletin*.

❧ Lesson 67 ❧

Don't Accept Someone's Views Just Because He or She Is Supposed To Be an Authority

I HAVE RECEIVED a great deal of good advice from authorities in my career, but some of the worst advice I have received has also been from people in positions of authority.

When I was interested in going to graduate school, I thought it would be a good idea to consult with my residential college dean regarding my future plans. (A residential college dean at Yale is in charge of providing career and other advice to several hundred undergraduate students.) I went to talk to the dean, and he welcomed me to his office. I told him I was thinking of going to graduate school. He told me that, basically, I was a technician, and that because I was a technician, I should go to a school of education, since schools of education train technicians.

I was crushed by his advice. Here I had hoped to receive encouragement, and all I received was what seemed like cruel discouragement. Fortunately, I did not listen to his advice and have had a more or less successful career in psychology. I also learned that one should welcome advice, but one also needs to evaluate the advice; then one needs to take responsibility for making the ultimate decision.

I have met so many people who have let offhand comments by persons in positions of authority destroy their possibilities. Don't be one of them. Make of yourself what you want to be.

❧ Lesson 68 ❧

Communicate Clearly

AN ATTRIBUTE of successful people in many fields is that they tend to be good communicators. If you look at the most famous psychologists, most of them are not only gifted scholars or practitioners, but also, good communicators as well. It therefore pays to develop your oral and written communication skills as much as you can. Some of the most well-known psychologists of our time, such as Steven Pinker, have developed their reputations not only because they are good scientists, but because they are especially effective communicators. On the contrary, people who have poor communicational skills may have wonderful ideas, but if they cannot communicate them, the ideas will be lost to others.

There are exceptions. Jean Piaget's writing is very dense and hard to follow but Piaget became one of the great psychological scholars of all time. However, Piaget's fame, at least in the United States, owes a great deal to effective communicators such as John Flavell who took up his cause, and wrote books and articles explaining Piaget's work. Most of us will not have others to interpret for us. It therefore behooves us to learn to write and speak effectively.

A few years ago I attended a conference of psychologists and two psychologists spoke in a symposium back-to-back on their work. One psychologist was a dynamic, effective communicator, who was enthusiastic about her work and showed it to the entire world. The second psychologist was at least as good a researcher—arguably, better—but spoke in a dry monotone voice that threatened to put much of the audience to sleep. After the symposium, it was the effective communicator who had streams of people coming up to talk to her. The other psychologist, whose work was really quite interesting, attracted few people. The work may have been interesting, but because she failed to communicate its interest and even sounded bored with it, she bored everyone else as well.

If your communication skills are lacking, it will pay off royally for you to work on improving them. There are books and courses available on improving both oral and written communication. As an academic, you will spend much of your time communicating. Learn how to do it well.

People sometimes think that it is one's ideas that are important, not the way one says them. Forget it. Most people are not willing to sit in their chairs and decipher cryptic messages. If the message is not clear, they will assume that is because the ideas themselves are not clear.

Communication skills include not only reading and writing, but listening. Being an effective listener can be one of the greatest assets you have. People have so much to tell you, if only you are willing to hear and then listen to what they have to say. To the extent this book has any good advice, it is largely because I have listened to the lessons that my mentors and colleagues have taught me.

❧ Lesson 69 ❧

Be a Little Ahead of Others, but Not Too Little or Too Much

TWO KINDS of contributions of which I think psychologists have to be wary are conceptual replications and what I call advance forward incrementations. Now let me explain what they are.

Conceptual replications help solidify the current state of a field (Sternberg, Kaufman, & Pretz, 2002). The goal is not to move a field forward so much as to establish that it really is where it is supposed to be. Thus, in science, if a finding is surprising, then a replication can help establish that the finding is a serious one. If the replication fails, then contributors in the field need to question whether they are where they have supposed themselves or perhaps have hoped themselves to be.

Conceptual replications are limiting cases in that they in some sense seem, at face value, to offer very little that is new in terms of the types of creative contributions that can be made. Yet such replications are important because they can help either to establish the validity or invalidity of contributions, or the utility or lack of utility of approaches, that have been offered.

For example, consider the choice reaction-time paradigm and its implications. As background, Jensen (1982) and others argued that correlations between scores on choice reaction-time tests and scores on intelligence tests suggest that individual differences in human intelligence could be traced to individual differences in velocity of neural conduction. Because tests of choice reaction time in no way measure neural conduction velocity, such interpretations of results were wholly speculative.

Vernon and Mori (1992) tested and seemingly confirmed Jensen's hypothesis. They developed a paradigm whereby they could measure speed of neural conduction in the arm. They found that neural-conduction velocity did indeed predict scores on conventional tests of intelligence. This was a startling finding because it suggested that what previously had been a speculative claim that at best was very loosely tied to data was instead a serious empirically supported claim. However, Wickett and Vernon (1994) later reported a failure to replicate this result so that its empirical status was cast into doubt. The Wickett and Vernon study was a replication study, and the failure to replicate arguably was as important to the field as would have been a replication. Failures to replicate can prevent a field from pursuing red herrings.

Work designed to yield exact replications and conceptual replications, where the generality of a finding or kind of product is assessed by trying to replicate it under circumstances somewhat different from those that originally gave rise to it, is about as unglamorous as any kind of work can be, it is necessary for the development of a field. Without conceptual replications the field would be (and probably often is) very susceptible to Type I errors (false alarms). In science, conceptual replications help ensure the solidity of the base of empirical findings upon which future researchers build. But researchers need to be careful of building careers on replications because they are considered perhaps the least creative type of contribution one can make. When one comes up for promotion or tenure, replications may not be as helpful as other kinds of research.

Advance forward incrementations occur when an idea is ahead of its time. The field is moving in a certain direction but is not yet ready to reach a given point ahead. Someone has an idea that leads to that point not yet ready to be reached.

157

The person pursues the idea and produces a work. Often the value of the work is not recognized at the time because the field has not yet reached the point where the contribution of the new work can be adequately understood. The creator accelerates beyond where others in his or her field are ready to go—often skipping a step that others will need to take. The value of the work may be recognized later than otherwise would be the case, or some other creator who has the idea at a more opportune time may end up getting credit for the idea.

For example, Alfred Binet is best known for his work on intelligence, but as pointed out by Siegler (1992), Binet did work on the nature of expertise in outstanding chess play and on the validity of eyewitness testimony. The work, which did not fit even remotely into existing paradigms of the time, was largely ignored. By the second half of the twentieth century, these and other topics that Binet had studied gained prominence. Binet, however, is virtually never cited in the current work on these topics.

Royer (1971) published an article that was an information-processing analysis of the digit–symbol task on the Wechsler Adult Intelligence Scale (WAIS). In the article, Royer showed how information-processing analysis could be used to decompose performance on the task and understand the elementary information processes underlying performance on it. Royer's work foreshadowed the later work of Hunt (Hunt, Frost, & Lunneborg, 1973; Hunt, Lunneborg, & Lewis, 1975) and my own work in particular (Sternberg, 1977, 1983), but his work went largely (although not completely) unnoticed. There could be any number of reasons for this, but one of the reasons is likely to have been that the field was not quite ready for Royer's contribution. The field and possibly even Royer himself did not recognize fully the value of the approach he was taking.

In my own career, I once did a grant proposal on concept naturalness. When I got the reviews back, they were rather negative, saying that the idea of naturalness of concepts was itself unnatural. I believe I was too early, or perhaps not persuasive enough, because a few years later, concept naturalness research was all the rage. Being too much ahead of your time can result in your getting credit later than you thought you would. But more often, it results in the person who had the idea at the "right time" getting credit.

So what should you do if you have an idea that is ahead of its time? The best thing you can do is to realize that you need not only to present the idea to your proposed audience, but *lead* the audience to it. In other words, you have to take them down the conceptual path that will prepare the audience for the idea: In essence, you reduce the distance between where their heads are and where you want their heads to be. You provide greater guidance to them in helping them to understand the idea than you would have if the audience had been ready for the idea. In this way, you can help them to understand and appreciate an idea that otherwise might have sounded so foreign to them that they could not use it.

☙ Lesson 70 ☙

Seek the Action in the Interactions

PSYCHOLOGISTS WASTE an inordinate amount of time seeking to answer questions such as "Is heredity or environment behind intelligence?" or more generally, "Is X or Y behind phenomenon Z?" Interactions often are the name of the game. For example, heredity and environment interact in the development of intelligence or almost anything else. A person with great genes brought up in a closet most likely will not develop into a brilliant scientist. Correspondingly, one has to have "healthy" genes to be able to benefit from an enriched environment. Someone born with a severe and incurable genetic disorder may not benefit from any environment, no matter how favorable it is.

There are countless examples of such false dichotomies. In the 1970s, when I was in graduate school, a big question was whether human information processing is serial or parallel. Another is whether human thought relies on images or propositions. These kinds of simplistic either–ors rarely help elucidate much about human thinking. Most psychological processes can be one thing or another, depending on the circumstances under which they are executed. Psychologists thus need to understand how structures and processes interact with the environment to produce the phenomena we observe in the world.

Anything can be carried too far. Interactions are so complex that one can get lost in them. Few studies have the power reliably to spot interactions beyond the third order. Science probably will never grasp all the complexities of human behavior. But it can go quite far with the techniques available to it. Thus, you want to recognize complexity but not allow yourself to become overwhelmed by it. Science is about reducing complex phenomena. It does not necessarily understand the full complexity of natural or other phenomena.

Keep in mind also that very few psychological phenomena are singly determined—meaning that they just have one cause and one cause only—and probably very few admit to no interactions. If we look at intelligence, personality, emotion, or motivation, each of them is complexly determined. Trying to find "the cause" of anything is likely to be a wild goose chase. Most things are multiply determined.

❧ Lesson 71 ❧

Seek Syntheses of Ideas That on the Surface Seem Incompatible

PEOPLE HAVE different styles of work. One style that has worked well, at least for me, is to synthesize ideas that in the past have seemed incompatible. For example, early in my career I was busy at work trying to synthesize what sometimes had been seen as two very different traditions in psychology, the cognitive–experimental tradition and the psychometric–differential tradition. The two traditions were often seen as incompatible because the former emphasizes understanding variation across stimuli or experimental conditions, whereas the latter emphasizes understanding variation across individuals. Cronbach (1957) pointed out that the two traditions are not necessarily incompatible, and he invited theory and research that would combine the two traditions. My early work (e.g., Sternberg, 1977, 1983) was one of several different attempts to forge the way toward such a synthesis. In other words I also have sought syntheses. For example, my work on thinking styles (Sternberg, 1997b) in some ways has provided a bridge between personality and cognition research. And my work on creativity has integrated aspects of cognitive, personality, and motivational research (e.g., Sternberg & Lubart, 1995).

I have found Hegel's (1931) notion of a dialectic particularly compatible with the seeking of psychological understanding. In a dialectic, an original statement, or thesis, is made regarding some topic. Sooner or later, it is countered by an antithesis, a statement that expresses, to a large extent, an opposing point of view. This statement is then eventually

162

superseded, at least according to some points of view, by a synthesis—that is, by an integration of the two positions that takes the best elements of both and throws away those elements that are ineffective. The dialectic points out that positions that may originally seem incompatible often later are found in fact to be compatible, sometimes through the realization that they deal with a given phenomenon or set of phenomena at different levels of analysis.

For example, I have proposed a theory of intelligence that posits analytical, creative, and practical abilities (Sternberg, 1985, 1997a), and Howard Gardner (1983, 1999) has proposed a theory of multiple intelligences according to which there is not one intelligence but rather there are 8 or possibly 9: linguistic, logical–mathematical, spatial, musical, bodily–kinesthetic, naturalist, interpersonal, intrapersonal, and possibly existential. At first glance, the two theories appear to be incompatible: Which is it, 3 or 9? But the theories also can be viewed as compatible and as analyzing intelligence at different levels. In particular, analytical, creative, and practical processing can be applied in any of the domains of Gardner's theory. For example, one can analyze a poem, write a poem, or read a poem so as to communicate its message—examples of analytical, creative, and practical processing applied in the linguistic domain.

The concept of dialectic applies in many ways. It applies to different theories. It applies to different paradigms. For example, behavioral and cognitive approaches to psychological phenomena were once viewed as competing with each other, but today, a cognitive–behavioral approach, at least to therapy, is among the most popular approaches available.

The dialectic also applies in the aspects of one's career that have little to do with the content of psychology per se. Very often, one will have to negotiate various things with other people—with advisors, with chairs of departments, with journal editors, with colleagues. Sometimes, the demands of one person seem utterly incompatible with the demands of another person. In my experience, however, constructive negotiations often reveal that all parties to an apparent conflict can be satisfied, at least to a first order of approximation. One should not assume that what one party wants cannot be made compatible with what another wants, even if initially it seems as though the demands or desires are incompatible.

Very early in my career, I saw myself as a sort of crusader against certain psychometric methods that were being used to study intelligence. I believed that I had better cognitive methods. Later in my career, I realized that my methods were not really better, but rather, just different. The best way to study intelligence was to combine the psychometric methods I had rejected with the cognitive methods that I originally thought had replaced the psychometric methods. Ideas that had originally seemed incompatible to me—as though one had to adopt one set of ideas or the other set—actually were quite compatible, and were stronger in combination than when considered separately.

✤ Lesson 72 ✤

Use Converging Operations

CONVERGING OPERATIONS refers to the use of multiple methodologies for studying a single psychological phenomenon or problem. The term was first introduced by Garner, Hake, and Eriksen (1956) in a path-breaking article on psychological methodology. The basic idea is that any one operation is, in all likelihood, inadequate for the comprehensive study of any psychological phenomenon. The reason is that any methodology introduces biases of one kind or another, and often, of multiple kinds. By using multiple converging methodologies (i.e., converging operations) for the study of a single psychological phenomenon or problem, one averages over sources of bias.

There are many examples of how converging operations can illuminate phenomena in a way that no one operation can. (See the original Garner et al. article for some such examples.) Often, new constructs are especially well served by such operations (Sternberg & Grigorenko, 2001).

Consider, for a first example, the construct of prejudice. Prejudice traditionally has been measured in one of two ways, either by a questionnaire asking participants to characterize their feelings toward groups of people (Allport, 1929; Dovidio & Gaertner, 2000) or by observations of behavior (Sherif, Harvey, White, Hood, & Sherif, 1961/1988). Many studies have shown that attitudes are often not particularly good predictors of behavior (e.g., Dovidio, Kawakami, Johnson, Johnson, & Howard, 1997). If one wished to understand prejudices, one would have to study both their verbally expressed attitudes and their actual behavior.

One could, of course, say that the crucial measure is behavior, and that the attitudes are only interesting to the extent they predict behavior. I disagree (see Sternberg & Grigorenko, 2001). Behavior is as interesting a predictor of attitudes as are attitudes of behavior. There is no ultimate dependent variable. Consider an example of this notion as it applies to attitudes and prejudices.

Recently, Greenwald, Banaji, and their colleagues (Greenwald & Banaji, 1995; Greenwald, Banaji, Rudman, et al., 2000) have developed measures of implicit attitudes that examine a wholly different aspect of how people feel about certain groups of individuals. These measures each are referred to as an Implicit Association Test, or IAT (Greenwald, McGhee, & Schwartz, 1998). The IAT is a computer-based reaction-time measure that provides an estimate of the degree of association between target concepts, such as attitudes toward African Americans and attitudes toward White Americans, and an evaluative dimension like pleasant–unpleasant. For example, African American faces are paired with "good" or "bad," as are White American faces. On half the trials, one pushes the same response key for "White" and "good," and on the other half, one presses the same key for "White" and "bad." The same holds for "Black" and "good" and "Black" and "bad." One can then compare the time it takes to associate good or bad with White or Black, respectively. The test provides a relative measure. In other words, a target concept (attitudes toward African American) must have a contrasting domain (attitudes toward White American). A participant's responses will indicate an implicit attitude toward African Americans relative to his or her implicit attitude toward White Americans.

Using such measures, these investigators have found consistently prejudiced implicit attitudes of White Americans toward African Americans and even often of African Americans toward African Americans. They have uncovered other negative implicit attitudes as well. Their measures of implicit attitudes correlate only poorly with the traditional measures of explicit attitudes, in which one simply asks individuals to state or rate their attitudes toward members of various groups. Thus, what result one gets depends on the dependent variable one uses.

The data suggest converging operations are needed if one fully wishes to understand people's attitudes toward various groups. One may wish to look at, for example, indicators of implicit attitudes, which usually involve timed decision tasks; measures of explicit attitudes, which typically take the form of questionnaires; and assessments of behavior. Ideally, one looks at all three.

Of course, there are many other examples of attitudes failing to predict behavior. Most people would agree that driving drunk is irresponsible, but a number of these people do it anyway. Many people who know that condom use may literally save their lives by preventing transmission of the HIV virus nevertheless fail to use condoms when they know they should. People who know that smoking is killing them continue to smoke. The examples are endless.

Another example of the need for converging operations can be seen in the study and measurement of intelligence and related intellectual abilities. Sternberg, Grigorenko, Ferrari, and Clinkenbeard (1999) used both multiple-choice and essay items to assess analytical, creative, and practical intellectual abilities. One of their analyses involved the use of confirmatory factor analysis by which they investigated, among other things, how effective the two item types (multiple-choice and essay) were in assessing the three different kinds of abilities. They found that the multiple-choice items were the more effective in assessing analytical abilities—the types of abilities assessed by traditional tests of intellectual skills—whereas the essay items were more effective in assessing creative and practical abilities. Using just one type of item (e.g., all multiple-choice or all essay) would have resulted in inferior measurement.

167

The principle of converging operations applies beyond the particular kinds of test items to the kinds of investigative operations used as well. The study of intelligence traditionally has drawn heavily on factor analysis. Carroll (1993), for example, followed in a long line of investigators who have developed and tested theories of intelligence largely or exclusively on the basis of factor analysis (e.g., Guilford, 1967; Spearman, 1927; Thurstone, 1938; see reviews in Brody, 2000; Carroll, 1982; Mackintosh, 1998; Sternberg, 1990). There is nothing wrong with factor analysis per se, but any single method has advantages and drawbacks. For example, factor analysis as typically used in the study of intelligence relies solely on the use of individual differences as sources of data. But many other useful sources of information can be drawn on to study intelligence, such as cultural analysis (Laboratory of Comparative Human Cognition, 1983; Serpell, 2000), cognitive analysis (Cooper & Regan, 1982; Deary, 2000; Estes, 1982; Lohman, 2000; Sternberg, 1982), and biological analysis (e.g., Larson, Haier, LaCasse, & Hazen, 1995; MacLullich, Seckl, Starr, & Deary, 1998; Vernon, 1997; Vernon, Wickett, Bazana, & Stelmack, 2000). These other methods of investigation can yield findings simply not susceptible to discovery by factor analysis, and in some cases, may call into question some of the results of factor analysis (e.g., Gardner, 1983, 1999; Sternberg, 1985, 1997a). My goal here is not to take a position on whether the results of factor analysis or any other single method, in particular, are right or wrong. It is simply to point out that converging operations can yield insights about psychological phenomena that are opaque to any single methodology.

If, as Garner, Hake, and Eriksen (1956) claimed, converging operations are so superior to single operations, why do some and perhaps many psychologists rely largely or even exclusively on a single method of analysis (or, for that matter, only two methods of analysis)? I (Sternberg & Grigorenko,

2001) believe there are three main reasons, none of them really acceptable from a research standpoint.

The first reason is *education*. Psychologists may have been educated largely in the use of a single methodology. They may have invested heavily in that methodology in their work. Learning how to do structural equation modeling or neural imaging or qualitative analysis, for example, can require a large amount of work, especially if one wishes to perfect each of the set of techniques. Researchers may seek to maximize the return on their time investment and to use what they have learned as much as possible. Even if they come to see the flaws of their preferred methodology, they may come to view the time invested as a sunken cost and seek to justify or even redeem the investment anyway. They thereby can become fixed in their use of single methods.

The second reason involves the notion of *panaceas*. Researchers can come to view a single methodology as representing a kind of panacea for the study of a certain problem or set of problems. At one time, some psychometric investigators saw exploratory factor analysis in this way, until its limitations became increasingly apparent (e.g., the existence of an infinite number of rotations of axes, all of which represent equally legitimate solutions statistically). To some of the same investigators as well as to other investigators, confirmatory factor analysis or structural equation modeling may have come to seem to be panaceas, although these methods also have their limitations, such as reliance on individual differences. Today, some scientists are viewing neural-imaging methods as a panacea. Some are busy compiling mental atlases that link certain areas of the brain to certain aspects of cognitive processing, often oblivious to the functional relations between the two and sometimes in the absence of an adequate theoretical foundation (see Sternberg, 2000). The truth is that no method will provide a panacea: Different methods have different advantages and disadvantages, and by using multiple methods one capitalizes on the strengths of the methods while helping to minimize the effects of their weaknesses.

The third reason involves *norms*. Norms of a field may also lead to methodological fixation. Some years ago, I submitted an article to one of the most prestigious psychological journals available. I was asked to revise the article, replacing regression analyses of the phenomenon under investigation with analysis-of-variance analyses. The request was odd because the two methods of analysis gave equivalent information (see Cohen & Cohen, 1983). But the norm of the journal was use of analysis-of-variance reporting, so I had to change my form of reporting. Fields, journals, and other collectivities develop norms that, to the members of those collectivities, may seem perfectly reasonable and even beyond question. These norms may become presuppositions of behavior that are accepted in a rather mindless way (Langer, 1997). The norms may lead investigators to do things in a certain way not because it is the best way, but rather, because it comes to be perceived as the only way or the only way worth pursuing. Norms should support, not undermine, converging operations.

❧ Lesson 73 ❧

Be Programmatic in Your Work

WHEN PSYCHOLOGY DEPARTMENTS make decisions about hiring, one of the things they look for in a candidate is not just a body of research, but also a program of research. A research program is an organized body and plan of research that seeks to develop a set of ideas to answer a set of questions that evolve, one from another. For example, in my own career I started off studying the information processing components of intelligence as it is traditionally defined (Sternberg, 1977, 1983). Then I began to believe that the traditional definition of intelligence is too narrow, because there are intelligent people who have little common sense, or what I called practical intelligence. Then I realized that some people were traditionally (i.e., analytically) and practically intelligent, too, but rarely or never seemed to have any meaningful ideas of their own. So I came to study creative intelligence and onward the research program went.

It is not necessary that all the research you do be programmatic. Many researchers, in the course of a career, come upon ideas that are distinct from any program of research, and pursue these ideas simply because they are interested in finding the answers. But, generally, the research with the highest payoff is that which falls into a programmatic line.

Sometimes, research that initially seems like it will be merely a sideline becomes a major program of research. In my own case, I collaborated with a student in a study of love (Sternberg & Grajek, 1984), expecting when I started this work to do just the one set of studies and not return to the topic. But I found that one idea led to another, and soon I was involved in a program of research that culminated in several books (e.g., Sternberg, 1998b, 1998c; Sternberg & Barnes, 1988).

Other times, research that you hope will lead to a full-fledged research program fizzles out. In the 1980s, I had some ideas about conflict resolution, and the ideas resulted in two publications in a well-known and well-regarded journal (Sternberg & Dobson, 1987; Sternberg & Soriano, 1984). I then had some other ideas, but I did not feel that there was anything particularly exciting about them. It seemed as though I had rather quickly reached a dead end. So I brought this incipient program of research to a close, at least temporarily. One rarely knows, in beginning a research program, whether it will prove to be highly productive or simply transitory. In this case, the research program proved to be transitory. Transitory research programs are fine, but ultimately, people who are remembered typically are those who have, at some point, established systematic programs of research.

❖ Lesson 74 ❖

Capitalize on Strengths; Correct or Compensate for Weaknesses

MOST PEOPLE are good at something, but almost no one is good at everything. The things that you are good at can make your career; the things that you are not good at can break it. It therefore is important to reach a self-understanding regarding your strengths and weaknesses.

Consider first the question of strengths. Some years ago I was listening to a well-known scholar give a talk, and I whispered to the woman sitting next to me that I thought the talk was particularly wonderful, and that I wished I could give a talk like that. She looked at me and said that I was wishing for the wrong thing—that I should wish that I could give a great talk in my own fashion. I realized that she was right. I should not be trying to be "great" in a way that works for someone else, but rather, in a way that works for me.

Consider next the question of weaknesses. I have had wonderful mentors—primarily Endel Tulving, Gordon Bower, and Wendell Garner—and at various points of my career have wished I could have the kinds of success they had. All three have won the APA Distinguished Scientific Contribution Award, all three are members of the National Academy of Sciences, and on and on their endless lists of scientific awards go. They fit my—as well as others'—prototypes of the most distinguished scientists. My work has taken me in different directions from theirs, and over the course of my career, I have had to come to terms with the fact that my career simply will not be like theirs. I think I have made good contributions, but they differ in various ways from those of my mentors.

173

Perhaps my contributions are more applied, or, some might say, less basic scientific. Whatever they are, they are different from Tulving's, Bower's, and Garner's.

We all need to come to terms with who we are and who we can be. Successful careers are not built on emulation of mentors. They are built on figuring out our strengths and weaknesses, and then making the best contributions we can make, given those patterns.

I admire and would like to be skilled at many kinds of work—highly sophisticated mathematical and biological work, for example. But, at least up to now, they are not for me. I suspect that many a career has failed on people's trying to be something they are not. This is not to say that we cannot develop a wide range of skills. Certainly we can. But for most of us, our profile of skills is not even, and we need to pin down what we do best.

In my own career, I have found a few things I do well. I enjoy inventing theories; I write prolifically; I typically give interesting talks; I love to mentor students. So I have made these cornerstones of my career. There are things I have found I do not do well. For example, I'm not one for formatting documents, I'm not good at little details, I have trouble sitting still in boring meetings. So I have tried to minimize the roles of these elements in my career. I have others format documents and, where possible, attend to little details. There are people who enjoy doing these things, and I enjoy working with them because they can do well what I do not do well. And I avoid committees unless I am really interested in them. When I have to serve on committees, I have learned to pay attention and try to take an active interest. I thus have tried, where I could, to capitalize on strengths and to compensate for or correct weaknesses. It has not always worked. But it's worked well enough for me to get by.

❧ Lesson 75 ❧

Concentrate on Comparing Yourself With Yourself Rather Than With Others

I BELIEVE THAT a serious mistake that some scholars make is to define themselves in terms of the extent that they one-up their rivals or even their colleagues. They get satisfaction not from excelling beyond their past selves, but from excelling beyond their real or imagined competitors. It is always tempting to compare oneself with rivals, but it is not a constructive way to build a career.

Just recently, I ate dinner with a famous psychologist. This is a person who by almost any objective standard has achieved a great deal of success. I was surprised to find this individual using much of the conversational time at the dinner knocking down the work of one person after another, and pointing out the ways in which his career has been superior to theirs.

We all have to make our own decisions, but my own feeling is that I would not want to live my life building up my own self-esteem by knocking down others. I think one can do one's best work if one asks how one can improve on one's past work, and not by worrying about how one compares with others.

I compete with myself. I think about my past work and how I can improve on it. There are always things you can do better. The best way to find them is to look at what you have done, reflect on what you could have done better, and then to use the lessons you have learned in your subsequent work. You will do your best work if you focus on competing with yourself rather than competing with others.

175

ROBERT J. STERNBERG

When I first taught introductory psychology, I was determined not to make the mistake my own intro teacher had made. He taught the course to students who had good memories. I had a lousy memory. But I like courses that appeal to creative thinking. So I started teaching the course in a way that appealed to students who liked to think creatively. I quickly saw that the course was bombing out. At first, I could not figure out why. Here I was teaching the course the way it should be taught, and it was not working. And then, I realized what I was doing wrong. I was making exactly the same mistake my own teacher had made: I was teaching to my own strengths. But those were not necessarily the strengths of the students in the class. To make the class a success I had to teach it to the wide variety of strengths of students in the class, not just to my own strengths. When I started teaching "triarchically"—to students with analytical, creative, or practical strengths (Sternberg & Grigorenko, 2000)—the course went much better. By competing with myself, and by learning from a mistake, I improved the way I taught.

❧ Lesson 76 ❧

Let Others Do Your Bragging for You

JOHN FLAVELL is one of the most distinguished cognitive–developmental psychologists of the generation ahead of me, and also one of the best liked. He is well liked for many reasons, but certainly one of them is his deep-seated and genuine humility. Although he is an icon of his time, I have never heard him brag or even recount his own impressive string of successes. In general, I have found the very best people in the field to be surprisingly modest. The second string often is not.

I know another psychologist who cannot seem to stop bragging. Much of her bragging takes the form of name-dropping. She manages to get into almost any conversation all of the important people with whom she has interacted. Even in meetings, she somehow manages to brag about the connections she has established. Perhaps she thinks she is impressing others. Mostly what people say of her is that she is a name-dropper. She seems to be the only one who is impressed.

In general, I think psychologists fare better when they concentrate on doing their best work rather than on bragging about how good their work is. If you do good work, others will spread the word for you. If you do not, no amount of bragging on your part is likely to make much of a difference.

❧ Lesson 77 ❧

Look for Collaborators With Whom the Whole Is More Than the Sum of the Parts

I HAVE WORKED in many different fields over the course of my career, and people sometimes ask me how I do it. One way is to have great collaborators. Over the years, I have been privileged to work with many wonderful collaborators—undergraduates, graduate students, postdoctoral students, and faculty members. Collaborators can be a key to your success. First, they will have ideas you will never think of. Second, they will stimulate you to have ideas you never otherwise would have had. Third, they will provide expertise you do not have. And fourth, they will make the job of doing research much more fun.

There are many projects that I never would have thought to have done without my collaborators. For example, in the late 1970s, I had two graduate students, Roger Tourangeau and Georgia Nigro, both of whom were interested in metaphor. I never had been particularly interested in metaphor. But they were, and so I let them lead me, in the same way that my own graduate advisor, Gordon Bower, often let his students lead him. The result was a series of papers on metaphor that were fun to work on and interesting to boot.

My collaborators and I have also done a number of international studies in exotic places, such as Jamaica, Kenya, and Tanzania. These studies have yielded some of our most important findings. For example, in Kenya, we found negative correlations between tests of academic and practical intelligence, a very important result for our research program (Sternberg, Nokes, et al., 2001). But we never could have done any of these international studies without a team of people at Yale and abroad who wished to be involved in the research. Those who do not collaborate miss one of the great joys and opportunities of an academic career.

❧ Lesson 78 ❧

Be Ethical All the Way

T HERE ARE MANY different temptations to be dishonest or otherwise unethical in an academic career. These choices are all losers.

The most obvious one is to fake data. If you really are tempted to fake data, you are in the wrong field. Consider another career, such as writing fiction. There just is no room at all for fudging or faking data in science.

First, once it starts, where does it stop? With one data point? With one article? With all the work you ever do? If you tell yourself you will only cheat once, you are probably like the hustler who will only hustle once. Once you cross the line, you're a faker, pure and simple.

Second, were you to think you would get away with it, it is harder to do than it looks. There are, of course, the blatant cases, such as people who use the same data points or figures and then claim that they are based on separate data collections. Moreover, people can and do request your data, and if there is something wrong with them, there is a good chance they will holler.

Third, the consequences of faking or fudging data are typically rather extreme, as in, your career is ruined. Who will want to hire you? Who will want to promote you? Who will want you as a colleague? And then, when you try to find another career, what do you tell people about why you left the first one? And if you lie, what do you do when they find out anyway? And what are you planning to do if or when the newspapers and magazines get hold of it, as they often do? I have read articles on alleged cheaters in *Science, The Chronicle of Higher Education,* and other sources mostly read by academics, but also in *The New York Times* and other national newspapers.

Finally, it is just plain unethical, so forget about it.

There are many other ways to be unethical. They are losers, too.

A second way is to tell a human-subjects committee which decided on whether your research is ethical that you will do one thing and then do another. Maybe the human-subjects committee is giving you trouble, or has given you trouble, and you figure that you can make life easier for yourself by "simplifying" for them—that is, by making it look as though you are doing anything other than exactly what you are doing. This is a really bad idea. First, participants sometimes complain, even with innocuous studies, and complaints trigger investigations. Second, word sometimes simply gets back, and if you are not doing what you said, or are doing what you did not say, that can cause trouble. Finally, human-subjects committees can check up on you if they wish, complaint or not.

If you are caught deviating from the approved protocol, a number of things can happen, all of them bad. The first is that the human-subjects committee can and probably will shut down your research project. The second is that they may shut down you, meaning they may shut down any other research projects you have, at that time or in the future. They may also investigate past projects for deviations. The third is that, if the deviation is serious, the complaint may go past the university to the funding agency. The federal government has been known to shut down all federally funded research in a university because of violations of human subjects requirements. This is bad for the university, and extremely bad for you, as your colleagues will be less than thrilled that your deviation shut them down. The fourth, which is even less fun, if that is possible, is that the newspapers may get hold of it, and then, good luck. This has happened to a number of investigators, and sometimes such news articles have even made the national press. It is great to make the national press, but not for violations.

A third way to be dishonest is to tell one colleague one thing and another colleague another thing. For example, you complain to colleague A about colleague X, thereby complimenting colleague A by taking him or her into your confidence. Then you proceed to complain to colleague X about colleague A, reversing the process. Or perhaps you merely tell one set of facts to colleague A and another set of facts to colleague X. People do these little kinds of deceits all the time. Why bother even to mention it? Because the assumption underlying such moves is that colleagues A and X are not talking and will never talk to each other, and that assumption is likely to be false. And as you do this to more and more colleagues, the chances of its getting around that you are deceitful begin to spiral. People then find out, sooner or later, that you are not to be trusted, and this is not a reputation you want to have in an academic career.

A fourth way to be dishonest is with regard to feedback. There are many ways to be dishonest about feedback. One is to review an article and praise an article you do not think is very good or pan an article that is good. Why would anyone do such ridiculous things? There are lots of reasons. Maybe you do not like the article, but a friend wrote it and you want the friend's work to be published. Or maybe the article's conclusions agree with your pet theory or pet findings and so you would like the article published so that your views are supported. Perhaps you do not like the person who wrote the article, and wish to use what you hope will be a rejection to get back at the author. Or you may not like what the results show, and so hope to keep the results out of the literature because the results do not match what your pet theory predicts. Or, even worse, maybe you hope to use the ideas yourself, and so pan the article in the hope that it will not get published and you can do a similar study.

There are many reasons why it is a bad idea to be dishonest in giving feedback. First, if you are the only reviewer to praise or pan an article, the editor and other reviewers may wonder whether you missed the point, or what your motivation is. You risk giving yourself a bad name. Second, if your comments simply do not jibe with what is in the article, you make yourself look stupid. Third, it is just plain wrong.

I think a prize for one of the stupidest cases of academic dishonesty I have seen in my career goes to an assistant professor who formerly was at my institution (although not in psychology) when I was an undergraduate there. This individual was very vocal on campus, constantly getting himself into the local news. One thing he did not do much was publish, however. Later, at least one reason why came out. It turned out that at the same time he held an appointment at my institution, he also held another full-time (and fully paid) appointment at another institution that was about an hour-and-a-half away. It turned out that he had been commuting between the two, never bothering to mention that he simultaneously held two full-time appointments. I know that my institution canned him, and I imagine the other one did the same.

Although this is the stupidest case of academic dishonesty I have been witness to, in earlier times, Cyril Burt reporting exactly the same correlations for data sets, as he added more and more data, was not one of the more clever examples of what appears to be academic dishonesty. And he studied IQ!

My experience in academia is that one can get by just fine being honest. There will be times when it may be embarrassing to be honest, as when you have screwed up. But, as some of the United States's past presidents have discovered, one deception tends to lead to another, which leads to another, and eventually you can end up in much hotter water than you started. In my experience, it is almost always the cover-up, not the original mistaken act itself, that really cooks people's gooses!

There is one guideline that I have sometimes found to be helpful in regulating my own sense of what is ethical. If something feels wrong, it probably is. My experience is that, when we cross the line, we usually know it, at least at some level. So keep track of your gut instincts. If something feels like it is cutting a corner, or like it is skirting the line of the ethical, it probably is. Find another, better path.

The bottom line is simple: Strive for ethical behavior.

❧ Lesson 79 ❧

Realize That Bad Times Come to an End

FOR BETTER OR FOR WORSE, you will always, in a career, end up having to do things you neither like to do nor do particularly well. In some periods, the bad things seem never to end. I am no great fan of long meetings, but I sit through countless long meetings. Sometimes I go through periods where it seems to be all meetings, all the time. You are best off recognizing the things that you don't like, and being reasonably cheerful about them. If you find this difficult, look at these undesired things as a tax you pay for being in a career you (hopefully) really enjoy. All jobs have such taxes: There is no perfect job. But just as you have to pay your taxes in full to the government, you have to pay your taxes in full to your job. Better times will come.

Sometimes you go through periods that are catastrophically bad. Everything seems to go wrong, perhaps in a short period of time. I've gone through several such periods. No matter what I did, it seemed to turn to crud. And what I didn't do—that turned to crud, too. At times I've wondered whether such bad periods would ever come to an end. They do. But hanging in, waiting for such periods to let up, can be very painful. Sometimes there simply is no substitute for patience and hope.

❧ Lesson 80 ❧

Fuse Teaching, Research, and Service

O PPORTUNITIES TO FUSE together teaching, research, and service are surprisingly abundant. Consider some possible combinations.

Teaching and research naturally go together. I have gotten several of my ideas for research from teaching. For example, some of my research has been on teaching introductory psychology, and the ideas for this research flowed from my having taught the course. Some of the research I have published has emanated from joint projects with students that started as course projects. And some of the courses I have taught have emanated from my desire to do research in an area and to understand the area better by teaching about it and by discussing it with students.

Teaching and service also can go together naturally. Many teachers use service projects as opportunities for students to learn about psychology in action. For example, when I took a course in child psychology as a student, many students spent at least some time observing or even working in day care centers to learn about what they are like. Service projects can also feed back ideas to students and faculty alike. Students may write reports based on their service experience, and faculty may be able to talk about service experience in their lectures.

Finally, research and service can go together as well. Service can lead to research projects, for example, on understanding factors that contribute to successful day care, or to adequate care in a homeless shelter. Research can also lead to service: Our studies of effects of parasitic infections on cognitive functioning of individuals in developing countries have led to treatment for such infections for many individuals who otherwise would never have been treated.

University service also can be useful to you. You may meet new people, and as a result, become involved in joint teaching ventures, joint research ventures, or simply conversations that feed into your teaching or research. Although service is not the primary way to get teaching or research done, it can help.

✣ Lesson 81 ✣

Know What Is Expected of You

Yale, like many comparable institutions, values both teaching and research, but as I have mentioned earlier, when the time comes for considering people for tenured positions, research typically counts substantially more than teaching. You probably will not get tenure if you are a particularly bad teacher, but you certainly will not get tenure if you are a particularly bad researcher, or are simply unproductive.

I have therefore always been surprised when, on hearing that they were being encouraged to move elsewhere, some assistant professors have moaned and groaned that they put all their time into teaching, and so it was not fair that they were being penalized for not getting more research done. There may have been any number of reasons for them to moan and groan, but that was not one of them. The reason is that the institution makes it clear in multiple ways that research is the main coin of the realm. So what was their problem? Deafness? Unwillingness to hear?

In the same way, other institutions may value teaching more than research, and dismiss faculty members with excellent research programs who are unable to teach students effectively. Because there is no one set formula across all institutions, one needs to learn a formula that works at the institution where one teaches.

Sometimes the priorities of the institution will be made as clear as day to you. Other times, they may not be quite so clear. There are several ways of finding out what the priorities are. One is to ask the chair or the dean. It is always better to ask, say, the department chair, in writing, perhaps in an e-mail, and then to get back a written answer. A second way is to ask colleagues who are not in administrative positions, although their responses will have less authority. A third way is to observe who has gotten tenure and who has not. If everyone or no one has, then you probably need not worry. Your fate is out of your hands. But if the proportion is somewhere between 0 and 1, you should find out what it is that the people who did (or did not) get tenure had in common, if anything. And a final way is to look at who seems to be rewarded by the department in informal ways. Which people are favored, and why?

❦ Lesson 82 ❦

Know the Rules, Regulations, Both Formal and Informal, That Affect You

I HATE READING RULEBOOKS and long lists of things I should and should not do. But, as noted above, these are times in which it really pays to know what is permissible and what is not. Stanley Milgram (1974) carried out experiments in which he pretended that participants were unmercifully shocking an individual (who actually was a confederate of the experimenter). Although the participants were debriefed, they had to live with the knowledge that they had administered what they had thought were painful electric shocks (even though they were no such thing). Milgram may have been able to carry out, at the time he was working, what today would be viewed by many as an ethically challenged set of studies. Current rules would not allow such a study, at least in the way it was done.

Times have changed for human-subjects committees. When I started my career, most applications were approved with what today would seem like a perfunctory review. Today, reviews are very careful and detailed. Times also have changed for grants. When I started my career, it was fairly common for people to be loose about what they charged to grants, and what activities they charged to which grants. Today, such looseness is no longer permissible. Many, perhaps most of our grants and contracts are audited, and one has to be prepared to justify every expense. It is totally impermissible to fund activi-

190

ties that should be occurring under one grant under another grant, or to fund activities that are far removed from what you proposed in the grant proposal.

Sometimes, the rules you need to follow are informal rather than formal. When I started my career as an assistant professor, classroom jokes with vague sexual innuendos were considered funny—at least, by most of the students. I would tell such jokes from time to time, and typically get laughter from the classroom. There came a time when, one day, a student raised his hand and accused me of making a sexist joke. I did not see it that way. I asked students to write me anonymously to say whether or not they thought the joke was sexist. Most did not, but, to my astonishment, a few did. The student who had raised his hand was not the only one.

From then on, I stopped telling jokes in class with sexual or other socially unacceptable innuendos. As the jokes were not "planned"—my sense of humor tends to be spontaneous rather than planned in advance—I had to be careful at first not to tell such jokes. After awhile, they simply disappeared from my repertoire. I realized that times had changed, and that I had to change with them. In the same way, professors have had to become much more careful in what they say to students, whether individually or in a group, so as to avoid charges or even the whiff of harassment of various kinds. In the course of a career, there are many ways in which one has to change. One either changes, or risks disaster. In my case, there was no formal rule—at least at the time—about what jokes were appropriate to tell. But there were informal rules, and I had to get with them!

❧ Lesson 83 ❧

Be Respectful and Pleasant Toward Others as Much as Possible but Don't Use Ingratiation

BEING VERY PLEASANT with people, civil toward them, and showing interest in them, their work, and their families typically does pay off. Many people do these things naturally. Others do not. In my experience, you should do these things if you at all have them in you to do. The field of psychology, like many other fields, is founded in part on personal relationships. People with better interpersonal relationships will thus typically be at an advantage over those with poorer ones. I doubt that good personal relationships ever got me a grant or a journal acceptance. But I'm quite confident that they helped. And being rude is always a mistake, regardless of the circumstances. I have found many people have long memories for rudeness, and it is not something for which you want to be remembered.

Some of the people at the very top of the field are not very good in personal relationships. If you make it to the top of the field, congratulations! You probably can afford to pay less attention to this advice than can some others. But very few people make it to the very top, and moreover, even those at the top still will be at an advantage if they treat others with respect and dignity.

When I was starting off my career, I was invited to give a job talk at an institution in which I was quite interested. I gave my talk, which I felt went rather well, and then invited questions. The question period was going fine when an individual, who looked like a beginning graduate student, asked a question that I thought was really pretty stupid. I was not about to tolerate stupid questions, so I gave what I thought was a clever, put-down answer. I later discovered that the "graduate student" actually was a remarkably well-preserved full professor in the program for which I was applying for a job. I didn't get the job.

In general, I have found that it *always* pays to treat people with respect, no matter who they are. I get e-mails from high school students that sometimes drive me up the walls. Many of them expect me to do their homework for them. But I try to answer them—very briefly—but politely. It just does not pay to be disrespectful of people.

You will get reviews of articles that seem to have been written by morons. At times, you may review articles that appear to have been written by morons. Resist the temptation to tell the authors what you think of them! *Never* make ad hominem criticisms. Criticize the work, not the person. There is no need in academia for people to be uncivil toward each other. If you are uncivil, you do not show yourself to be clever but rude. People will think more highly of you if you keep the level of discourse professional and avoid personal attacks. And you will get better outcomes in all aspects of your career.

I recently got a review of a paper I coauthored in which the reviewer said I should consider doing research in an area that is more consistent with the level of mental ability I bring to bear upon the task of research. I laughed when I saw the comment, although I must admit it stung. But I had seen similar savage reviews before, and was not about to let the reviewer's personal hostility upset me. Such comments, directed against people earlier in their careers, can be devastating, however. Really, no one has the right to make such comments, and it was, in my opinion, a mistake for the editor even to have circulated them.

Although you want to be respectful, you don't want to be ingratiating. Ingratiation is a delicate topic in academia. To what extent do you suck up to those in authority to curry favor? Or should you do it at all?

When I was an assistant professor, I was in the office of a fellow assistant professor discussing something or other. I do not remember what, because during the discussion, I happened to see the colleague's date book open, and in it, the names of virtually the entire senior faculty, who had been invited to dinner on different days. I thought to myself. "Oh no! I didn't know I was expected to invite all of the senior faculty to dinner. Now what?"

I never did invite the entire senior faculty to dinner. It just wasn't "me." Later, I got tenure and the other faculty member did not. So the dinner invitations perhaps did not pay off as the colleague had hoped. My experience is that blatant flattery of everyone around in positions of authority typically is seen as such, and does not produce very good results, except to label the individual engaging in it as a "suck-up."

At the same time, it does pay to point out to people that you recognize their strengths and their contributions. That is not ingratiation. It is fair game. People often feel under valued in academia. As I have said before, there seems to be much more negative feedback than positive feedback. So by all means, if you like what someone does, tell him or her. The individual will be glad to hear it, so long as it is sincere.

❧ Lesson 84 ❧

Learn To Tolerate Ambiguity

THERE ARE PERIODS in your life when you may try to do something in a new way. You may be trying to come up with an idea for a new experiment, or an idea for a new way of teaching, or a new way of organizing courses in a department. When you are trying to do things in a new way, there often is a period in which you do not quite have the new idea "just right." Such periods—when you know that the old way of doing things will no longer work, but when you do not quite have the new way down pat—create feelings of ambiguity and hence feelings of stress. It is like an old vinyl record that is caught between two grooves and is not in either one of them. You may be tempted, in such periods, to give up on your plans to do things in a new way, and to go back to your old and suboptimal way of doing things. But you are better off tolerating the ambiguity long enough to get it right, even though such tolerance of ambiguity is very difficult.

At Stanford, I did my first-year project under Gordon Bower on a topic called negative transfer in part–whole free recall. The details of the paradigm and study are unimportant. But the project was successful. It largely resolved a puzzle in the literature. At that point, I realized that there was a disadvantage to resolving a puzzle. There was no work left to be done on the puzzle. So I had to find a new area in which to do research.

I had come to graduate school hoping to study intelligence, and it seemed like this was my chance to get into intelligence research. But I just could not come up with an idea I liked. I remember going to meet my former undergraduate advisor, Endel Tulving, at the Center for Advanced Study in the Behavioral Sciences. I met with some of his distinguished colleagues for lunch and told them that my first-year project had gone well, but that I was not sure what I wanted to do next. I remember their looking at me with what, at the time, seemed to be pity. Here I was just having finished my first year of graduate school, and I already was washed up. At that point, I thought that maybe I just couldn't stand it any longer. Maybe I should just find some other problem in memory to study, which would be easier for me to do than to find a problem in intelligence. After all, I had done several studies on memory, and should be able to find one more to do.

I decided instead to tolerate the discomfort of this ambiguous period. One day I was looking at materials that my wife (at the time) was using called "People Pieces." I saw a way to use them to make analogies, and so came to me the idea for my first study in graduate school on intelligence. I tolerated the ambiguity long enough to get to where I needed to be, and thereby ended up working on problems about which I cared more rather than on problems about which I cared less.

❧ Lesson 85 ❧

Don't Shoot Your Mouth Off

I HAVE A COLLEAGUE on a committee on which I serve who constantly is shooting his mouth off. The minute he disagrees with someone, he says so without thinking through what he says. The minute he is upset with someone, he finds a way to shoot a barb at the person. He appears to be very pleased with his ability immediately to attack anyone who displeases him. But he seems to be unaware of the fact that others have long ago stopped liking him and even taking him seriously. They are so offended by his aggressive behavior that even when he makes good points, people often do not listen to him.

We all know people who shoot their mouths off. In this case, the result was a loss of credibility. The consequences can be greater or lesser, but, in my experience, they are never good. If you feel the urge to make a "killer" remark, at least think a few minutes before making it, or at minimum, count to 10! Learn to listen. Give others a chance to speak as well.

❧ Lesson 86 ❧

Know When To Move On in Your Work and When Not To

I ONCE WAS ATTENDING a conference where there was a presentation by a colleague at another university who was about 10 years post-PhD. The presentation was on her attempts to prove a certain thesis. The problem was that she had been trying for the entire 10 years of her career to prove this thesis, and her research program was going nowhere. Yet she would not give up. I don't think her career has gone very far. Perhaps she is still trying to prove the same thesis.

There is a fine line between perseverance and perseveration. Perseverance occurs when you keep trying to reach your goals in the face of obstacles. Perseveration occurs when you keep trying to reach your goals, in the absence of any evidence, over a period of time, that these goals are getting any closer to being reached. You need to know when to give up.

Sometimes you give up for a given time. For years, I was interested in studying wisdom, but could not find an angle. I had some tentative ideas about ways of approaching the problem, but they did not seem to lead very far. I began to see that my attempts were getting me nowhere, so after one or two such attempts, I decided to put the study of wisdom aside and move on to other things. Some years later, I saw what I thought was an avenue of research for studying wisdom, and I again started actively studying it. But I was glad I had left time to incubate on the problem, because I just was not ready to study it earlier on.

❦ Lesson 87 ❦

Control Self-Pity

THERE ALMOST CERTAINLY will come times in your career when things seem to be going wrong, even horribly wrong. You may get one rejection after another, you may have a death in the family, you may go through a messy divorce, you may become seriously ill, your children may be in trouble, you may have legal problems, and on the list goes. Moreover, it may even be that you have several of these things going wrong all at once. Unfortunately, you are not alone. In most lives, there come periods of time when nothing seems to go right.

I think that these periods are often the times that distinguish those who ultimately succeed to their levels of aspirations from those who do not. Most of us stagger or blunder through such periods and find it difficult, or even impossible to work. I've been through such periods myself and wondered how I would ever get through them. But these periods do come to an end, if only you can see your way through them, and once they do, it is important to get back to work. Indeed, working on teaching, research, or administration through such periods may even help you get through them. It also helps to have a close network of friends. The important thing is not to let yourself become derailed.

I must admit I have felt sorry for myself at times. But then I've tried to move on. Working has been a much better way of handling distress than has been ruminating. It is one thing to reflect, another to ruminate. Reflection probably helps; rumination just drives you further toward the pit of despair.

⚜ Lesson 88 ⚜

Love It or Leave It

MOST PEOPLE go into academia because it is what they love. Others go into it because it is what they think they love. They then find out they were mistaken. What do you do if you found you have made a mistake, perhaps even a horrible mistake?

Obviously, we all have to decide the answer to this question for ourselves, but in my opinion, the best thing to do is get out if at all possible, the sooner the better. Sometimes graduate students drop out of our graduate program, and they may be perceived as "losers" by those who still are in the program. In my opinion, their dropping out shows the exact opposite. They have recognized that what they are doing is not the right thing for them, so they find something else to do. This is exactly the right attitude to have. If you are in the wrong business, find one that will make you happy. The extrinsic rewards of academia are not so great that, if you are unhappy with your situation, it is worth staying in the career. Find something else to do that better enables you to make the most of your strengths.

When I was a graduate student, there was a very successful fellow student who stayed at Stanford for one year, and then dropped out to go to law school. He could have been a very successful psychologist, I think, but it wasn't for him. Today he is a famous constitutional lawyer. He did what he needed to do, as should we all.

❧ Lesson 89 ❧

Check Your Work

O NE OF THE EASIEST things you can do is to check your work, but it is also one of the things that people seem most loath to do. Nevertheless, there are few things you can do that require less work and that have higher payoff for the time invested.

Whether you are a student or a professional, few people like to read work that is not proofread. Professors may give you a lower grade: They have many papers to read, and often do not react well to sloppiness or repeated grammatical or other mistakes. Reviewers of articles submitted for publication are even less friendly to poorly presented papers. They are reviewing the papers as a service to the field, not because they have to review them. So they often react negatively when they are repaid for their generosity by a poorly written or badly mangled paper. I have sometimes refused to read such papers. I have returned them to the editor and said that I did not think it a fair use of my time to correct multiple errors of typography that the author should have corrected. Such errors include not only errors of spelling and grammar, but multiple missing pages of text or word-processing errors whereby one is reading one part of a paper when, suddenly, the text shifts to a totally different part that should have been placed elsewhere.

I thus strongly encourage you to proofread all your work, as I have proofread this manuscript. Proofreading does not guarantee that you will fix all errors. Sometimes, you can look at an error multiple times and not see it, simply because it is *your* error. But, in general, you will do yourself and your reputation a favor if you are careful about your work.

When I suggest you check your work, I am talking about checking "within reason." A real career-killer is super-perfectionism. There are some people who are never ready to let go of anything. They need to check their work, and then check it again, and then keep checking it, just to make sure. By the time they get around to sending a paper out for publication, someone else has already beaten them to the punch and done something similar. It is important to check your work, but not to the point of obsession. Find the "golden mean." Do not hang onto things so long that by the time you let go of them they have lost much of their value.

❧ Lesson 90 ❧

Ask Colleagues for Informal
Comments on Your Work

RELATED TO THE NOTION of proofreading is the notion of seeking informal feedback. I have found, countless times, that colleagues will discover errors, even blatant errors, that I never would have noticed in my work. Sometimes the errors are ones that I would have been downright embarrassed for others to have noticed. Other times, I have not sought informal collegial feedback and have regretted it when I received negative comments from reviewers that I am certain could have been avoided had I first gotten informal feedback.

When you hear your voice on a tape recording, it often does not sound like you. It sounds like someone else speaking. Which is the way your voice sounds, the way you hear it or the way it sounds on tape? The way it sounds on tape, of course. Because you are both speaking and listening, there is a distortion in what you hear. The same is true when you do work. Because you both write it and evaluate it, there is bound to be some degree of distortion. Others can help you get through this distortion, and see things you never would see if left to your own devices.

❧ Lesson 91 ❧

Ask About the Best and Worst Possible Outcomes Before You Even Begin

S OMETIMES, STUDENTS or colleagues come to me with ideas that, to me, do not seem very appealing. But I recognize that the fact that an idea does not seem appealing to me means nothing more than that—namely, that it is not appealing to me. Others, perhaps many others, may love the idea. When I am skeptical about an idea, say, for a research project, I sometimes ask the colleague or student what he or she views as the best and worst possible outcomes of the proposed work. If the success of the entire project hinges on a single test of statistical significance, for example, the individual might want to think carefully about investing major amounts of time or resources, especially if there is no strong evidence that the test will come out the way one hopes it will.

I personally do not like "all-or-none" kinds of projects and try to avoid them. I mean by an "all-or-none" project one that either comes out exactly the way I had hoped for or else it is a loss. I try to build features into studies so that if one thing does not work out, something else may. For example, I may add additional dependent variables so that if the first dependent variable does not yield significant results, another one may. Or I may add an independent variable so that if I do not get a main effect I hoped for, I may nevertheless get an interaction.

The stakes are different at different points in a career. If you are tenured, you probably easily can take larger risks than if you are not. In any case, you always need to look at the cost–benefit ratio for the projects you undertake, and if

204

the costs are especially great, consider whether the benefits outweigh them.

One kind of risk you never should take is an ethical one. Do not count on not getting caught. The times are such that there is extremely low tolerance for ethical lapses in all areas of academia and in society in general. For example, lapses in following human-subjects protocols that at one time might have been tolerated and largely ignored today are noticed and dealt with accordingly. Standards for sexual behavior also have changed. For example, my own university fairly recently passed a regulation forbidding intimate personal relationships between faculty and the students whom they supervise. The point is that ethical lapses are extremely risky and a poor idea.

In making all these points, I should make one thing clear again, as I have before. I am not claiming to be perfect—far from it. I have made many mistakes, perhaps more than my share. But we all need to learn from experience, and I have tried to do so.

❖ Lesson 92 ❖

Realize That Sometimes the Reason We End Up Doing Things Is Not the Reason We Started Doing Them

I ONCE WAS TALKING to a colleague in another country who had emigrated from the United States and gone to live abroad. I asked him whether he had fulfilled his goals in moving—if the move had brought him whatever it was he was seeking. He commented that the reasons one went to live in the country often were not the reasons one decided to stay, and that one had to decide, having lived there for a number of years, whether it was a good move or a not so good one. Those who decided it was a not so good one either lived in a state of dissatisfaction, or went back to the United States.

It occurred to me that his comments were a good lesson that applied in many contexts. Often the reasons for which we undertake the things we do in our careers are not the reasons for which we continue to do them. For example, whenever I have undertaken an administrative responsibility, I have found the job to be full of surprises, not all of them pleasant. When I have undertaken research projects, often they have come out in ways that were totally different from all of the outcomes that I thought were possible. When I have taught new courses, I have sometimes been surprised at the reactions of students to various exercises I had planned, with some working much better and others working much worse than I had expected. In each case, I started doing something for one reason, and then had to decide whether to continue doing it when I realized that the reason for which I had undertaken what I was doing no longer applied.

I think that flexibility here, as in many things, is of key importance. Research projects sometimes have come out better than I ever thought possible, not because they worked out as I expected, but because they worked out in some entirely different way. Being director of graduate studies for our department had some unexpected pains, but many unexpected joys. The bottom line is that you need continually to be reassessing what you are doing and why you are doing it, and make the most of the opportunities available to you.

❧ Lesson 93 ❧

Redefine Yourself
as Often as You Need To

S OME YEARS BACK a very famous cognitive psychologist came
to give a talk at our institution, and before his talk, we
were sitting in my office chatting. I had just had a cognitive
psychology text come out, and perhaps that is the reason that
the conversation turned to cognitive psychology and our roles
in it. For whatever reason, he commented to me: "But you're
not a cognitive psychologist anymore, Bob." I was crushed. I
had been trained by Endel Tulving and then Gordon Bower,
had always defined myself as a cognitive psychologist, and
was very disappointed to learn that a pre-eminent cognitive
psychologist did not even consider me as one of the brethren
anymore! I don't think he meant to be hurtful. I think he was
just saying what he thought, and that just upset me more.

The more I thought about it, however, the less dis-
turbed I was. My work had indeed taken me into a number
of different directions, and whether or not I was a cognitive
psychologist, I certainly had ceased to be a traditional cognitive psychologist. Traditional cognitive psychologists do not
study love, for example.

I came to believe, and still believe, that labels can be
as harmful as they are helpful. They are helpful, perhaps, to
give others a quick idea of the kinds of problems you choose
to study. But they can be harmful in limiting your own definition of yourself and what you do. You can end up letting the
label limit you and effectively dictate what you can and cannot
do. For example, if you define yourself as a cognitive psychologist, you may immediately decide that love is outside the

208

purview of what you can study and if you define yourself as a social psychologist you may decide that problem solving is outside the range of phenomena you can study.

I think it important to concentrate on finding interesting problems, whatever they may be, rather than to concentrate on fulfilling a set of roles specified by a label. I therefore encourage students and colleagues to follow their dreams rather than be limited by largely arbitrary labels.

❧ Lesson 94 ❧

Do Not Assume That Good Ideas Sell Themselves: Sell Them

EVERYONE WOULD LIKE to assume that their wonderful, creative ideas will sell themselves. But as Galileo, Edvard Munch, Toni Morrison, Sylvia Plath, and millions of others have discovered, they do not. On the contrary, creative ideas are usually viewed with suspicion and distrust. Moreover, those who propose such ideas may be viewed with suspicion and distrust as well. Because people are comfortable with the ways they already think, and because they probably have a vested interest in their existing way of thinking, it can be extremely difficult to dislodge them from their current way of thinking.

One of the first colloquia I was invited to give was at a well-known testing company. I was very excited about the opportunity. I thought that this talk would be a great chance to show people at this company that they were on the wrong track in understanding intelligence. To my surprise, the talk did not go particularly well at all. In retrospect, I don't know why I thought it would. After all, this was an organization that had become extremely wealthy on the basis of conventional ideas about abilities. Why should they believe me? And moreover, what did I expect—that senior, established people in the field would hear me, curse themselves for having wasted their careers, and then become devotees of mine? Not realistic! I needed to sell them on my ideas, not expect they would buy into them because they were good, or at least because I thought they were good. When you have creative ideas, remember they generally will not sell themselves. You must sell them.

210

❧ Lesson 95 ❧

Strive for Impact

EVERY ONCE IN AWHILE, I am asked what I am trying to achieve in my career. Chances are, you will be asked too, at some point. Although you obviously do not have to answer the question, it might be worthwhile to consider if you do have any higher order goals, and if so, what they are.

I do have a higher order goal, which is to strive for impact—on science, on education, and on society. The center I direct at Yale, the PACE Center, is motivated by a goal of making a difference. Indeed, for me, the meaning that life has is that the world be a somewhat different place for one's having been in it. I do not claim this is the meaning everyone should assign. Perhaps the answer to the question of life's meaning given in the science fiction novel *The Hitchhiker's Guide to the Galaxy*—"42"—is just as good!

My own satisfaction is directly related to the impact I can have. For some people societal goals will be less important. They may decide that their goals begin and end with science. When I look at the power science has to be used for either good or for evil, I believe that all of us should consider adding society to the equation. The development of wisdom in people seems not to have kept up with the development of technology, and society desperately needs for wisdom to catch up, before it destroys itself. Before September 11, 2001, such words might have seemed Cassandra-like and perhaps unnecessarily pessimistic. Today they perhaps seem more realistic. The world is what we make it, and we can make it better or worse as we choose.

❧ Lesson 96 ❧

Seek To Be Remembered for Your Positive, Not Negative Contributions

DURING MY FIRST YEAR as an assistant professor, I became interested in a problem that my faculty mentor, Wendell Garner, was studying, namely, whether structure is in the stimulus or in the interaction between people's perception of the stimulus and the actual stimulus. I believed then, and believe now, that structure is in the interaction. Garner, however, was to some extent a follower of Jimmy Gibson, the great psychologist of perception, and believed that large amounts of structure reside in the stimulus.

I did a study that I thought was a nice demonstration that Garner was wrong. The study did not directly support the interactionist position, but did seem to me to undermine the stimulus-based position. I wrote up the article, criticizing Garner's position on the basis of my data. That was a pretty gutsy thing for me to do, given that Garner was a senior faculty member and also chair of the department!

I submitted the article to a journal, and it got rejected. Not letting myself be fazed, I presented the contents of the article as a talk to the group of Saul Sternberg (no relation to me) at Bell Labs in Murray Hill, NJ. After the talk, Sternberg raised a point regarding my data that I had missed. This was the one time in my life—at least so far—that a comment just utterly demolished a talk. I realized that he was right, and that my data actually showed nothing at all. I was totally humiliated and only wished that I would instantly disappear.

No trap door opened, and Sternberg was very kind and genial about the whole thing. I went back and felt a need to apologize to Garner, because of course he knew about the work I was doing. A lesser scholar and a lesser person would have held what I did against me. He didn't. Instead, he told me, in his avuncular style, that I had an important lesson to learn, namely, that scientists are judged primarily by the positive contributions they make, not by the negative ones. This was great advice.

There are some people who try to build a career attacking others. In essence, they try to ride on the coattails of others, hoping to attract attention to themselves by attacking people, usually ones who are considerably better known than they are. I have had the honor of being attacked by several such people over the course of my career. I say "honor" because these people do not bother to attack you unless they think you are well enough known to bring them attention. In essence their careers are parasitic in that they prey on those who are well known to become more well known themselves.

After Garner gave me his advice, my whole attitude toward the field of psychology changed. I realized that the attack dog mentality really does not bring one very far. Moreover, as Kuhn (1970) pointed out, new paradigms tend to replace old paradigms not when the old paradigms are merely criticized, but when there are better or at least more currently useful ideas to take their place.

This is not to say that you should never criticize anyone's research. Part of almost any research career will involve disagreeing with other people. The important thing is to have a better idea yourself—something that replaces or builds on what they have done.

❧ Lesson 97 ❧

Invent Your Own "Game"

I HAVE BEEN TOLD that Paul Torrance, a famous psychologist in the field of creativity, would advise his students to invent their own game. By that he meant that creative individuals are not ones who follow the career paths of others, but rather, people who invent their own career path. I believe that this is very good advice.

My own career path has been traditional in some ways, untraditional in others. It is traditional in that I went to college, then graduate school, then to a job, interrupting my educational stream by only a semester to work in the Yale admissions office. But my career has been untraditional in other ways: for example, in the range of problems in psychology I have chosen to study (including, among other things, intelligence, creativity, wisdom, thinking styles, love, hate, and conflict resolution). My choice of research topics has never been governed by fads: I tend to study problems that relatively few other investigators study.

I have sometimes felt that I have paid a price for my unconventional career. I do not fit neatly into any one special interest group, so I always feel somewhat on the outside. Or it may just be my nature to feel as though I am on the outside. If I had to redo my career, however, I would not change that choice. I created my own game, have enjoyed the game, and have been willing to pay any price for inventing the game. And there have been many advantages too: There always will be some people who will respect you more, not less, if you go your own way.

When I speak of inventing your own game, I wish to make it clear that I am referring to how you go about your work, not to how you relate to other people. The one kind of game you want to avoid is the game you play with other people. When you play games with other people, you may think they do not notice. But the chances are they do. And the chances are that, in the long run, they will want to have as little to do with your games as possible. One of the characteristics I value most in people is that they are straight with me, and forego game-playing. So don't waste your time playing games with people. Instead, invent your own game in your work, and then play that game to the hilt.

✧ Lesson 98 ✧

Realize That in the Short Run, the Payoffs Often Are for Ideas and Work That Do Not Threaten Anyone, but in the Long Run, the Payoffs Often Are for Ideas and Work That Do

ONE ISSUE you may have to deal with in the course of a career is that of work that threatens other people. For example, in my own career one of the main topics I study is intelligence. I believe that unitary theories of intelligence (centered on a so-called general factor—g—of intelligence) are not fully adequate. There are many people in the field who particularly like unitary theories and who believe me to be wrong. There are some among them who feel threatened by people who disagree with them, just as I am susceptible to feeling threatened by people who disagree with me. And sometimes people who feel threatened, for whatever reason, turn nasty.

My advice is to get used to it. No matter how polite you are, no matter how willing you are to see other sides, if you take a stand, you will find at least some people ready to be antagonized. Backing down does not always help. Some people go away when you back down; others, sensing weakness, attack even harder, figuring you will not have the guts to oppose them. I thus believe that you have to stand for what you believe in, and let the chips fall where they may.

As president of the American Psychological Association, I have to deal with this kind of issue all the time. There are people in the association who disagree with me strongly on many issues. Some of them are very powerful in the association, and a few are perhaps less scrupulous than I ideally would have hoped for. When I face opposition from them, there is a loud voice in my head that tells me I am hitting my head against a wall. But I believe I need to stand up for what I believe in, and take the flak. That's what I believe I was elected to do, and that's what I will do, uncomfortable though it may be.

❧ Lesson 99 ❧

To Persuade Is as Important as To Inform

I SOMETIMES SAY, only half-jokingly, that almost every business involves sales in some way. How does an academic career in psychology involve sales? Well, some of us spend much of our time giving talks, writing articles, and writing grant proposals to persuade people to see things the way we do. Whenever I give a talk, I realize that my audience has heard or will hear many people who disagree with what I have to say. It is my job, in part, to persuade them to see things in my way, at the same time that I recognize that, ultimately, the choice is theirs.

The difference between the typical soap salesman and me, I believe, is that the product I sell is my own and I truly believe, at some level, in what I say. I say "at some level" because, as I mentioned earlier, I know that no scientific theories represent a final word. But I believe my theories and work have something to offer and I would like people to believe at least in aspects of them. So I recognize that, whenever I write or speak, I am trying to persuade as well as to inform.

I do not necessarily want people to believe everything I say. Ultimately, I expect they will combine my ideas with the ideas of other people and with their own ideas to come up with a synthesis that works for them. But I do hope that my ideas will be part of that synthesis.

❧ Lesson 100 ❧

Deal With the Impossible Problem of Assassins

THERE IS ONE THING we all hope will not happen to us in our career but that may in fact happen, and that is that we acquire an "assassin" who is out to do us in. Sometimes, for whatever reason, someone decides he or she has it in for us, and then that person just will not let go. It seems as though the person's mission in life is to bring you down.

I wish I had wonderfully insightful advice to give regarding how to handle this problem, but I do not. Sometimes talking to the person helps; sometimes it does not. If you have a common superior, talking to the superior may help, but it may not, and in rare cases, may hurt if it gets back to the assassin. Fighting fire with fire usually does not help either; it just gives you, as well as the assassin, a bad reputation. Talking about what is being done to you risks just spreading rumors that you would prefer not to spread. Ignoring the person may work, and is in my experience usually the best way to handle such problems. Probably each case has to be handled on its own merits. But you should be aware that such things do happen, regrettable though they may be.

❧ Lesson 101 ❧

Do Not Put Off Your Personal Happiness Forever: Enjoy Your Life

THERE IS ALWAYS more to do in an academic career—a class not yet prepared for, an article not yet written. This fact creates a problem.

As an undergraduate, you may choose to work very hard so that you will get into a good graduate school. Thus your personal life may have to be placed on the back burner. As a graduate student, you will want to get through your dissertation and get a good job, so you will need to work very hard. You may therefore decide to delay personal satisfactions. As an assistant professor, you will want promotion to associate professor, and possibly promotion to tenure. Then you will want promotion to full professor, because you will not want what for some would be the embarrassment of ending your career as an associate professor. And then, as a professor, you may wish to get an endowed chair. And of course, there are always honors you have not yet won that are out there to be won.

My point is that if you choose to delay personal happiness and satisfaction, you may end up delaying forever. A career is important, but for most of us, it is not a full life. You need to find other things in your life. In my own case, I have studied two foreign languages as an adult, learning one to a high level of mastery and the other to a very crude first level. I have even started playing the cello again.

220

When I was in college, I stopped playing the cello. I had been first cellist in my high school orchestra and was dejected when, in college, it was clear that I would be, at best, in the middle of the pack. I reasoned that if I was not going to be a really good cellist, then why even bother? So I quit. Throughout most of my adulthood, I defined myself as an "ex-cellist."

Then, at the age of 48, I realized that I did not have to define myself as an ex-cellist, and that this definition of myself was preventing me from playing again. My old cello was long gone, so I bought a new one. And I started playing and enjoying the cello again. I realized that it is not important for me to do everything really well. If I'm a rather mediocre cellist, well, so what? I'm not trying to be Yo-Yo Ma. Insisting to myself that I be the best only hurt me in my opportunity to do something I enjoy.

Similarly, you need to pay attention to your significant other, your children, and others who matter in your life. Have I always been successful in doing so? No. But I have learned that in the long run, few things are more important. Someday, my work will be gone and I will be gone, and what will live on after me will be my two children and their children. They are perhaps the most important things I've had some hand in creating.

So work really hard, but don't let your work be your life. There is so much to enjoy in life and so little time in which to enjoy it. Make your life what you want it to be.

✣ Lesson 101 ½ ✣

Don't Just Read It, Do It

I HOPE you have benefited from the lessons in this book. So here is my last piece of advice: Don't just read it, do it! Your life is yours to live as you wish. I hope the knowledge I have gained through the years will help you make the very best possible of your career and your life. Good luck!

References

Allport, G. W. (1929). The composition of political attitudes. *American Journal of Sociology, 35,* 220–238.

Argyris, C. (1999). *On organizational learning* (2nd ed.). Boston: Blackwell.

Brody, N. (2000). History of theories and measurements of intelligence. In R. J. Sternberg (Ed.), *Handbook of intelligence* (pp. 16–33). New York: Cambridge University Press.

Carroll, J. B. (1982). The measurement of intelligence. In R. J. Sternberg (Ed.), *Handbook of human intelligence* (pp. 29–120). New York: Cambridge University Press.

Carroll, J. B. (1993). *Human cognitive abilities: A survey of factor-analytic studies.* New York: Cambridge University Press.

Cohen, J., & Cohen, P. (1983). *Applied multiple regression/correlation analysis for the behavioral sciences* (2nd ed.). Hillsdale, NJ: Erlbaum.

Cooper, L. A., & Regan, D. T. (1982). Attention, perception and intelligence. In R. J. Sternberg (Ed.), *The handbook of human intelligence* (pp. 123–169). New York: Cambridge University Press.

Cronbach, L. J. (1957). The two disciplines of scientific psychology. *American Psychologist, 12,* 671–684.

Deary, I. J. (2000). Simple information processing. In R. J. Sternberg (Ed.), *Handbook of intelligence* (pp. 267–284). New York: Cambridge University Press.

Dovidio, J. F., & Gaertner, S. L. (2000). Aversive racism and selection decisions: 1989 and 1999. *Psychological Science, 11,* 315–319.

Dovidio, J. F., Kawakami, K., Johnson, C., Johnson, B., & Howard, A. (1997). On the nature of prejudice: Automatic and controlled processes. *Journal of Experimental Social Psychology, 33*(5), 510–540.

Ericsson, K. A. (1996). The acquisition of expert performance: An introduction to some of the issues. In K. A. Ericsson (Ed.), *The road to excellence: The acquisition of expert performance in the arts and sciences, sports, and games* (pp. 1–50). Mahwah, NJ: Erlbaum.

Estes, W. K. (1982). Learning, memory, and intelligence. In R. J. Sternberg (Ed.), *Handbook of intelligence* (pp. 170–224). New York: Cambridge University Press.

Flynn, J. R. (1999). Searching for justice: The discovery of IQ gains over time. *American Psychologist, 54,* 5–20.

Gardner, H. (1983). *Frames of mind: The theory of multiple intelligences.* New York: Basic.

Gardner, H. (1999). *Intelligence reframed: Multiple intelligences for the 21st century*. New York: Basic.

Garner, W. R., Hake, H.W., & Eriksen, C. W. (1956). Operationism and the concept of perception. *Psychological Review, 63,* 149–159.

Gilovich, T., Vallone, R., & Tversky, A. (1985). The hot hand in basketball: On the misperception of random sequences. *Cognitive Psychology, 17*(3), 295–314.

Gould, S. J. (1981). *The mismeasure of man*. New York: Norton.

Greenwald, A. G., & Banaji, M. R. (1995). Implicit social cognition: Attitudes, self-esteem, and stereotypes. *Psychological Review, 102*(1), 4–27.

Greenwald, A. G., Banaji, M. R., Rudman, L. A., Farnham, S. D., Nosek, B. A., & Rosier, M. (2000). Prologue to a unified theory of attitudes, stereotypes, and self-concept. In J. P. Forgas (Ed.), *Feeling and thinking: The role of affect in social cognition. Studies in emotion and social interaction, second series* (pp. 308–330). New York: Cambridge University Press.

Greenwald, A. G., McGhee, D. E., & Schwartz, J. L. K. (1998). Measuring individual differences in implicit cognition: The implicit association test. *Journal of Personality and Social Psychology, 74*(6), 1464–1480.

Guilford, J. P. (1967). *The nature of human intelligence*. New York: McGraw-Hill.

Hegel, G. W. F. (1931). *The phenomenology of the mind* (2nd ed.; J. D. Baillie, Trans.). London: Allen & Unwin. (Original work published 1807)

Hunt, E., Frost, N., & Lunneborg, C. (1973). Individual differences in cognition: A new approach to intelligence. In G. Bower (Ed.), *The psychology of learning and motivation* (Vol. 7, pp. 87–122). New York: Academic.

Hunt, E. B., Lunneborg, C., & Lewis, J. (1975). What does it mean to be high verbal? *Cognitive Psychology, 7,* 194–227.

Jensen, A. R. (1982). Reaction time and psychometric g. In H. J. Eysenck (Ed.), *A model for intelligence*. Heidelberg: Springer-Verlag.

Kuhn, T. S. (1970). *The structure of scientific revolutions* (2nd ed.). Chicago: University of Chicago Press.

Laboratory of Comparative Human Cognition. (1983). Culture and cognitive development. In P. Mussen & W. Kessen (Eds.), *Handbook of child psychology* (pp. 295–356). New York: Wiley.

Langer, E. J. (1997). *The power of mindful learning*. Reading, MA: Addison Wesley Longman, Inc.

Larson, G. E., Haier, R. J., LaCasse, L., & Hazen, K. (1995). Evaluation of a "mental effort" hypothesis for correlation between cortical metabolism and intelligence. *Intelligence, 21,* 267–278.

Latané, B., & Darley, J. (1970). *The unresponsive bystander: Why doesn't he help?* New York: Appleton-Century-Crofts.

Lohman, D. F. (2000). Complex information processing and intelligence. In R. J. Sternberg (Ed.), *Handbook of intelligence* (pp. 285–340). New York: Cambridge University Press.

Mackintosh, N. J. (1998*). IQ and human intelligence.* Oxford: Oxford University Press.

MacLullich, A. M. J., Seckl, J. R., Starr, J. M., & Deary, I. J. (1998). The biology of intelligence: From association to mechanism. *Intelligence, 26*(2), 63–73.

Milgram, S. (1974). *Obedience to authority: An experimental view.* Harper Collins.

Royer, F. L. (1971). Information processing of visual figures in the digit symbol substitution task. *Journal of Experimental Psychology, 87,* 335–342.

Seligman, M. (1998). *Learned optimism.* New York: Pocket Books.

Serpell, R. (2000). Intelligence and culture. In R. J. Sternberg (Ed.), *Handbook of intelligence* (pp. 549–580). New York: Cambridge University Press.

Sherif, M., Harvey, L. J., White, B. J., Hood, W. R., & Sherif, C. W. (1988). *The Robber's Cave experiment: Intergroup conflict and cooperation.* Middletown, CT: Wesleyan University Press. (Original work published 1961)

Siegler, R. S. (1992). The other Alfred Binet. *Developmental Psychology, 28*(2), 179–190.

Simonton, D. K. (1997). Creative productivity: A predictive and explanatory model for caret trajectories and landmarks. *Psychological Review, 104,* 66–89.

Spearman, C. (1927). *The abilities of man.* London: Macmillan.

Sternberg, R. J. (1977). Component processes in analogical reasoning. *Psychological Review, 84,* 353–378.

Sternberg, R. J. (Ed.). (1982). *Handbook of human intelligence.* New York: Cambridge University Press.

Sternberg, R. J. (1983). Components of human intelligence. *Cognition, 15,* 1–48.

Sternberg, R. J. (1985). *Beyond IQ: A triarchic theory of human intelligence.* New York: Cambridge University Press.

Sternberg, R. J. (1986). *Intelligence applied: Understanding and increasing your intellectual skills.* San Diego: Harcourt Brace Jovanovich.

Sternberg, R. J. (1990). *Metaphors of mind: Conceptions of the nature of intelligence.* New York: Cambridge University Press.

Sternberg, R. J. (1997a). *Successful intelligence.* New York: Plume.

Sternberg, R. J. (1997b). *Thinking styles.* New York: Cambridge University Press.

Sternberg, R. J. (1998a). A balance theory of wisdom. *Review of General Psychology, 2,* 347–365.

Sternberg, R. J. (1998b). *Cupid's arrow: The course of love through time.* New York: Cambridge University Press.

Sternberg, R. J. (1998c). *Love is a story.* New York: Oxford University Press.

Sternberg, R. J. (1999a). A propulsion model of types of creative contributions. *Review of General Psychology, 3,* 83–100.

Sternberg, R. J. (1999b). The theory of successful intelligence. *Review of General Psychology, 3,* 292–316.

Sternberg, R. J. (2000). *Making school reform work: A "mineralogical" theory of school modifiability.* Bloomington, IN: Phi Delta Kappa Educational Foundation.

Sternberg, R. J. (2001). Why schools should teach for wisdom: The balance theory of wisdom in educational settings. *Educational Psychologist, 36*(4), 227–245.

Sternberg, R. J. (2002a). Everything you need to know to understand the current controversies you learned from psychological research: A comment on the Rind and Lilienfeld controversies. *American Psychologist, 57*(3), 193–197.

Sternberg, R. J. (Ed.). (2002b). *Psychologists defying the crowd: Stories of those who battled the establishment and won.* Washington, DC: American Psychological Association.

Sternberg, R. J. (Ed.). (2002c). *Why smart people can be so stupid.* New Haven, CT: Yale University Press.

Sternberg, R. J., & Barnes, M. (1988). An introduction to the psychology of love. In R. J. Sternberg & M. Barnes (Eds.), *The psychology of love* (pp. 3–10). New Haven, CT: Yale University Press.

Sternberg, R. J., & Dobson, D. M. (1987). Resolving interpersonal conflicts: An analysis of stylistic consistency. *Journal of Personality and Social Psychology, 52,* 794–812.

Sternberg, R. J., Forsythe, G. B., Hedlund, J., Horvath, J., Snook, S., Williams, W. M., et al. (2000). *Practical intelligence in everyday life.* New York: Cambridge University Press.

Sternberg, R. J., & Grajek, S. (1984). The nature of love. *Journal of Personality and Social Psychology, 47,* 312–329.

Sternberg, R. J., & Grigorenko, E. L. (1995). Styles of thinking in school. *European Journal for High Ability, 6*(2), 201–219.

Sternberg, R. J., & Grigorenko, E. L. (2000). *Teaching for successful intelligence.* Arlington Heights, IL: Skylight Training and Publishing Inc.

Sternberg, R. J., & Grigorenko, E. L. (2001). Unified psychology. *American Psychologist, 56*(12), 1069–1079.

Sternberg, R. J., & Grigorenko, E. L. (in press). *Intelligence applied* (2nd ed.). New York: Oxford University Press.

Sternberg, R. J., Grigorenko, E. L., Ferrari, M., & Clinkenbeard, P. (1999). A triarchic analysis of an aptitude-treatment interaction. *European Journal of Psychological Assessment, 15*(1), 1–11.

Sternberg, R. J., Kaufman, J. C., & Pretz, J. E. (2002). *The creativity conundrum: A propulsion model of kinds of creative contributions.* New York: Psychology Press.

Sternberg, R. J., & Lubart, T. I. (1995). *Defying the crowd: Cultivating creativity in a culture of conformity.* New York: Free Press.

Sternberg, R. J., Nokes, K., Geissler, P. W., Prince, R., Okatcha, F., Bundy, D. A., et al. (2001). The relationship between academic and practical intelligence: A case study in Kenya. *Intelligence, 29,* 401–418.

Sternberg, R. J., & Soriano, L. J. (1984). Styles of conflict resolution. *Journal of Personality and Social Psychology, 47,* 115–126.

Thurstone, L. L. (1938). *Primary mental abilities.* Chicago, IL: University of Chicago Press.

Tulving, E. (1966). Subjective organization and effects of repetition in multitrial free-recall learning. *Canadian Journal of Psychology, 19,* 242–252.

Tulving, E. (1981). Similarity relations in recognition. *Journal of Verbal Learning and Verbal Behavior, 10,* 479–496.

Tulving, E., & Thomson, D. M. (1973). Encoding specificity and retrieval processes in episodic memory. *Psychological Review, 80,* 352–373.

Tversky, A., & Kahneman, D. (1973). Availability: A heuristic for judging frequency and probability. *Cognitive Psychology, 5,* 207–232.

Vernon, P. A. (1997). Behavioral genetic and biological approaches to intelligence. In H. Nyborg (Ed.), *The scientific study of human nature: Tribute to Hans J. Eysenck at eighty* (pp. 240–258). Amsterdam, Netherlands: Pergamon/Elsevier Science, Inc.

Vernon, P. A., & Mori, M. (1992). Intelligence, reaction times, and peripheral nerve conduction velocity. *Intelligence, 16*(3–4), 273–288.

Vernon, P. A., Wickett, J. C., Bazana, P. G., & Stelmack, R. M. (2000). The neuropsychology and psychophysiology of human intelligence. In R. J. Sternberg (Ed.), *Handbook of intelligence* (pp. 245–264). New York: Cambridge University Press.

Wickett, J. C., & Vernon, P. A. (1994). Peripheral nerve conduction velocity, reaction time, and intelligence: An attempt to replicate Vernon and Mori. *Intelligence, 18,* 127–132.

Zuckerman, H. (1983). The scientific elite: Nobel laureates' mutual influences. In R. S. Albert (Ed.), *Genius and eminence: The social psychology of creativity and exceptional achievement* (Vol. 5, pp. 241–252). New York: Pergamon.

Index